GREEK MUSIC
FOR GUITAR

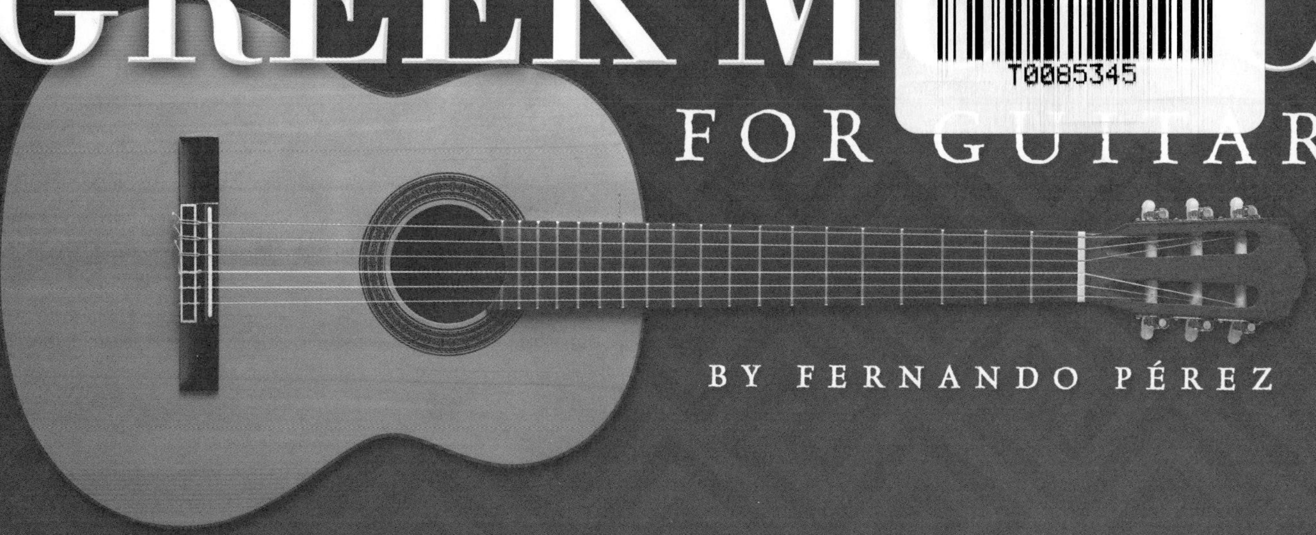

BY FERNANDO PÉREZ

To access video, visit:
www.halleonard.com/mylibrary
Enter Code
7020-6488-7433-9431

ISBN 978-1-4803-9531-2

HAL•LEONARD®
CORPORATION
7777 W. BLUEMOUND RD. P.O. BOX 13819 MILWAUKEE, WI 53213

In Australia Contact:
Hal Leonard Australia Pty. Ltd.
4 Lentara Court
Cheltenham, 3192 Victoria, Australia
Email: ausadmin@halleonard.com.au

CONTENTS

INTRODUCTION

In your hands is a book compiling some of the coolest and most enjoyable Greek music styles. After years of studying this music and other related styles, I wanted to create a repertoire truly faithful to the Greek tradition that was worthy of the guitar's unique capabilities. This meant I had to pay close attention to the details of Greek music while building guitar arrangements that were musically interesting and technically accessible.

I have always believed a musician must learn something new in every piece of music he or she studies. In my opinion, this is the key to growing and becoming a well seasoned musician. Finding ways to make the pieces interesting to you will also help your audience stay interested in your musical work. Now I am presenting to you the results of my efforts, hoping I have achieved this goal. Once you have learnt this repertoire, I encourage you to try adding your own embellishments and other ideas to the pieces to really make them personal to you. Even better—try creating your own compositions.

All the music in this book can be played on nylon- or steel-string guitars. They'll both sound different, so the choice is just one of personal preference.

Whichever you choose, I sincerely hope you enjoy and learn much with this book. Ultimately, I hope this music will bring you closer to and make you fonder of one of the many wonderful cultures living on this planet: the Greeks.

Fernando Pérez
Heraklion, Greece
February 2015

ABOUT GREEK MUSIC

Greece is an incredible place for music. Geographically located in an area known as "the gateway between East and West," it's influenced by two of the major musical systems in the planet: the Western music system and the Middle Eastern one (also known as the world of Makam.)

Exploring this country's music, one can find a great diversity of rhythms, scales, and chord progressions. From the melodies found in the well-known Bouzouki as well as in Cretan Lyras and Lautos, to the intricate rhythms of the touberleki as we approach the Balkanic areas, it is truly diverse. Besides these, the influences from the Byzantine and Ottoman cultures are still palpable. The country's musicians seen to be divided into two main schools: those who study the Western musical system and those who have been brought up with music in the Middle Eastern tradition. You find both types of musicians playing the same recognizable melodies but with a unique sound.

To learn either system thoroughly takes a big effort and years of study. For this reason, it's rare to find a musician who really knows both well. Although the country may be divided between these two, they get along and complement each other well.

Being familiar with Greek instruments and how they are played is important in understanding the music. This is especially true when dealing with the guitar.

The guitar in Greece still has a limited use. Most traditional Greek music guitarists use the instrument in a basic way, strumming, arpeggiating chords or picking a melody. Except a very few exceptions there is no real Greek music made for guitar. By saying Greek music made for guitar I am referring to music based on the traditional styles but fully arranged for a guitar, like the works we find in classical or fingerpicking guitar music where the player is able to play bass lines, melodies and harmonies all at a time. So in order to truly create this music for the guitar, we need to know not only the musical system but the instruments originally used to play it.

On the guitar, we will follow the approach found in Flamenco music—another style based on Middle Eastern music. This is to say that we are going to move around in different keys using the capo—even if it would be possible to play the music without its help. This is because many traditional instruments don't work for certain keys. It is this "handicap" that shapes the performance and final sound in this style of music. Using the capo on the guitar to switch between certain keys will give us the feeling that we are almost as limited as the traditional instruments, and this will help us to more closely emulate their sound.

In the scores, you will find many ornaments applied to the principal notes. Although these are written in Western classical notation, pay close attention to the video recording for proper performance. If possible, listen to traditional Greek music played on original instruments to hear how these ornaments are supposed to sound. Keep in mind we are trying to imitate these instruments with the guitar.

We'll also try to imitate the tone of certain instruments on the guitar. For example, in styles using a clarinet to play melodies, we can imitate its sound by playing more "sul tasto," which means playing with your right hand closer to the fretboard. To imitate the bouzouki, we can do the opposite by playing "ponticello," or close to the bridge. When copying the lauto or lavta, play more with your right-hand thumb plucking up and down, as if you were using a pick, rather than plucking with your index, middle, and ring fingers.

MELODIES AND SCALES

Greek melodies are based on a few scales. They are not difficult at all, but the key is to understand their behavior. The melodic tendency is modal and follows many of the guidelines found in Middle Eastern modal music—also known as Makam music.

For instance, one of the most common scales found in Greek music is what we call in the West a Dorian augmented fourth scale. This is a basic Dorian mode with a raised 4th (#4), hence the name. In the Makam tradition would be something close to what is called Makam Nekriz.

Here is a Dorian ♯4 in the key of E.

Example 1

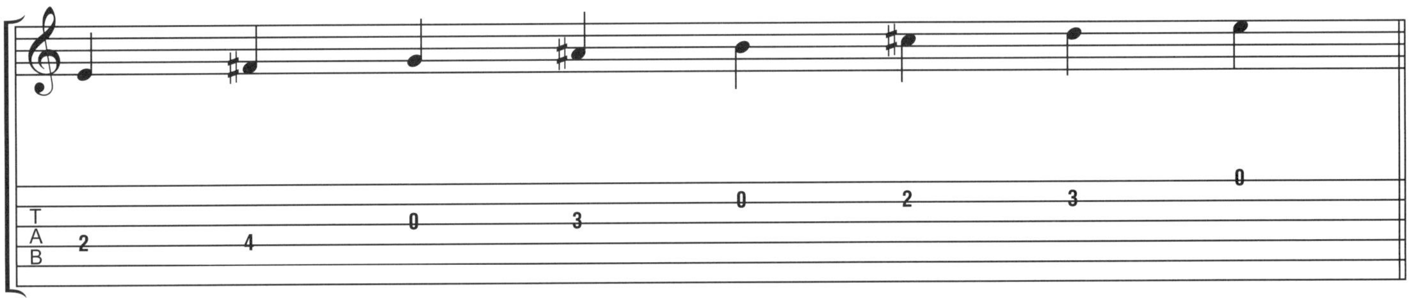

In Oriental music, very often we find a scale-mode starting with a half step interval followed by one and a half step plus another half step. This is the typical sound we always use to evoke Arabic, Turkish, or even Indian music.

Example 2

These four notes create the beginning of what is known in the Western world as a Phrygian major mode. But in Greece, it is used as an influence coming from the Turkish music, also known as Makam music. These Makams don't have an easy explanation, but for now, let's say they are like a musical mode with many rules shaping them.

The above tetrachord, which we call Phrygian major, in Turkish and Arabic music is known as Hijaz. Widely known in the Middle Eastern music world, this tetrachord is used in the West to evoke any music which should have a Middle Eastern flavor.

Now, Greek music is part of the gate between East and West. There we find sounds that are truly from the East but at the same time sound close to the West. It is the case of this Dorian ♯4 scale where we find the Phrygian major, or Hijaz, tetrachord between the second and fifth notes.

Example 3

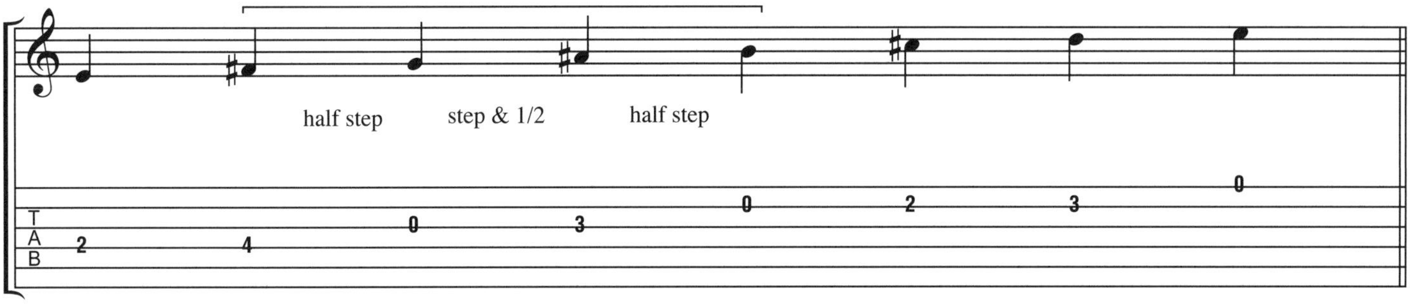

The fact that we find this tetrachord in the middle—and not at the beginning—of the scale helps to smooth the sound. That is why we can hear its flavor but not as strongly as with an original Middle Eastern scale. This is an important thing to keep in mind when we want to compose or improvise our own original music and give it a Greek flavor.

Let's look now at another detail happening in melodies. As we learn the tunes in this book, or any other Greek music, we will notice a strange behavior of the scale. This is best demonstrated with an example. Check out the last notes of the scale coming from the 5th up to the octave.

Example 4

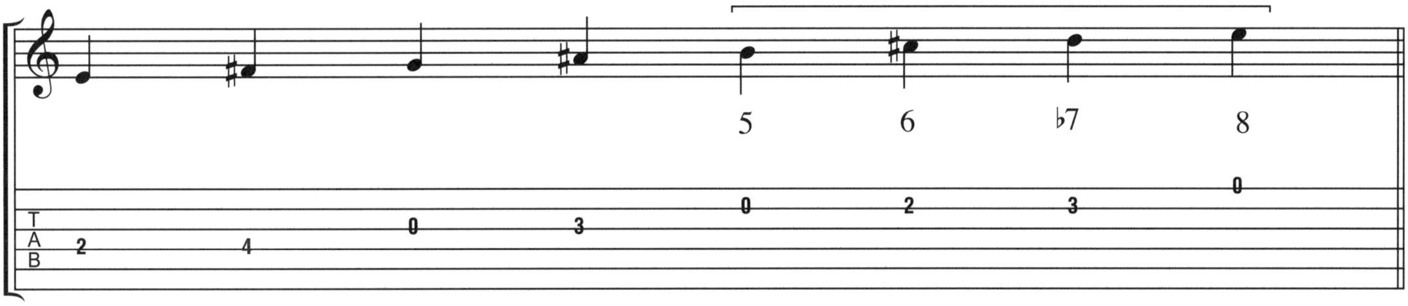

We have written this last tetrachord of the scale as 5, 6, ♭7, and 8. But after learning this scale, we will find that, in many occasions, the ♭7th turns into a natural 7th. Which one is better: the ♭7th or the natural 7th? Both maybe? If so, when do I use one or the other?

First, let's see where this comes from. As mentioned above, Greek music is very much influenced by Makam music coming from Turkey and the Middle East. In this musical system, we find a very interesting effect happening. There is a flowing force in the melody that's very important to keep in mind when we play. In this case, we will find melodic phrases coming from lower notes with an ascending flowing force. In some instances, these phrases will not aim to reach the octave. In these cases, we use the ♭7th. Every time this happens, after the ♭7th, we should continue in a descending way. To help you understand this, try to picture yourself playing with a ball, throwing it up towards the ceiling but never touching it. The highest point the ball reaches is the ♭7th, and right after that, it starts to descend. It is just a natural physical law.

Now sometimes the melodic phrase will want to reach the octave—either to stay there or pass over it and continue in the higher octave. You can think of this as throwing the ball much stronger to reach the ceiling and even break through it.

This phenomenon is known in Middle Eastern music as the *ascending-descending attraction.*

Let's look at this phenomenon from a different perspective. Imagine you are standing on the roof with your ball tied to an elastic rubber string.You throw the ball down through the hole in the ceiling you just made from downstairs, and it comes back up by the action of the elastic string. Every time you throw down the ball, it passes the hole, but it doesn't descend much further. This is because of the elastic string's attraction that pulls it back up. If we translate this into music, the ceiling/roof is the octave. The melody has arrived there and wants to stay. It can move up freely, but there's a tendency for it to go back down if we play too low below the octave; in reality, we want to stay in the higher octave. So we need to play the natural 7th under the octave, because the b7th would want to descend down again.

Try the next example. Observe where you are in the melody: E is 1, F♯ is 2, G is 3, and so on. Take special note of the 6, ♭7 (D), 8 (E), and natural 7 (D♯) and how they relate to one another depending on the direction of the melody. Be aware of the ascending-descending attraction.

Example 5

We can find a similar behavior with the fourth note. Usually, we use an augmented 4th (♯4) because it leads the melody to the 5th. But in some compositions, we play the natural 4th to develop the melody there. Just as we saw in the octave, the 5th becomes the central resting point.

Not only do we find the natural 4th instead of the augmented, but also the minor 3rd (♭3) can become a major 3rd in order to create the ascending-descending attraction with the natural 4th. Let's say we are playing a melodic phrase starting on the first note of the scale; it may go something like this.

- It moves up around the first three notes, sometimes passing through the augmented 4th leading us to the 5th.
- Once it goes back down, we want to move to a natural 4th, creating the usual cadence going from a tonic/stable feeling to a subdominant/less stable feeling (I say "less stable" because the dominant would be "unstable"). So the melody moves to the natural 4th, making its base or resting point there.
- It moves up a little and goes back to the natural 4th, and when we want to descend only slightly beneath the natural fourth, we do it using the major 3rd, which leads us back to the natural 4th.
  Once we are ready to descend back to the first note of the scale and its surroundings, we change to the minor 3rd (♭3) to create an attraction towards the first note.

Try the next example. Observe where you are in the melody; are you on the 1, 2, ♭3, 4, or 3? Be aware of the ascending-descending attraction.

Example 6

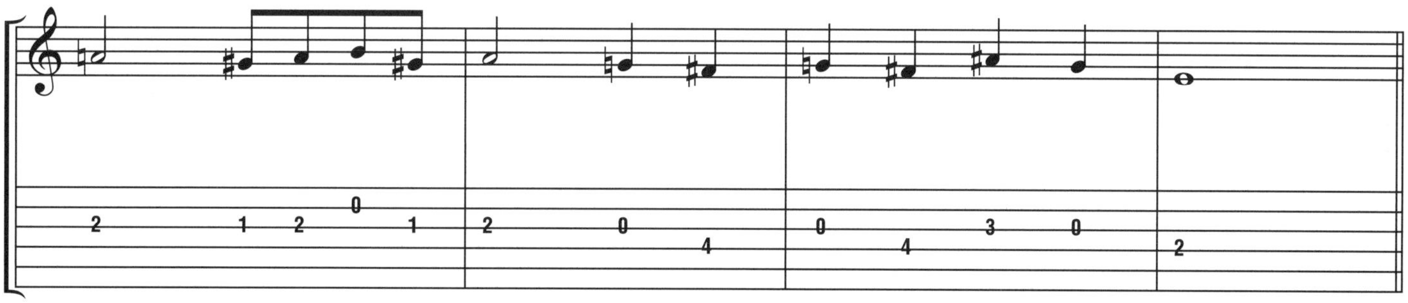

Other scales to be found in Greek music behaving as modes are the Aeolian mode (or natural minor scale), harmonic minor, and Phrygian major. There are also many tonal tunes using the major scale.

Since this is not a full theory book, I have just showed the Dorian ♯4 in order for you to understand the ascending-descending attraction behavior also found in other scales or modes.

HARMONY AND CHORD PROGRESSIONS

Harmony in Greek music is very straightforward. Since harmony doesn't exist in Middle Eastern music, most chord progressions are very typical cadences from the West and easily recognizable. Sometimes when we listen to Greek tunes, we might find a clash between the sound of chords played in Western instruments and the sound of certain notes in the traditional instruments with Middle Eastern origins. This is because the latter are able to play what we call *microtones* or *quarter-tones*. These microtones are notes tuned slightly different than the ones found in Western instruments. When an instrument is playing chords based on Western tempered notes and another is playing a melody which includes these microtones, we experience sound clashing.

Here is an example of a typical chord progression found in styles like Hasapiko, Hasaposerviko, or Syrtaki.

Example 7

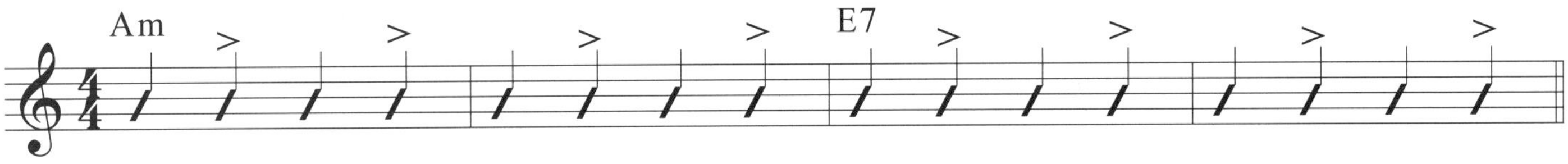

It is interesting to notice how chord progressions change when we work on music styles from areas closer to the Balkans. In the next case, the chord progression starts using a lot of diminished sounds. At times, it's difficult to recognize if a chord is minor or diminished, as it bounces often from one to another. Also the i (tonic minor chord) to V7 (dominant chord) progression changes to i and ♯IV diminished chords.

Example 8

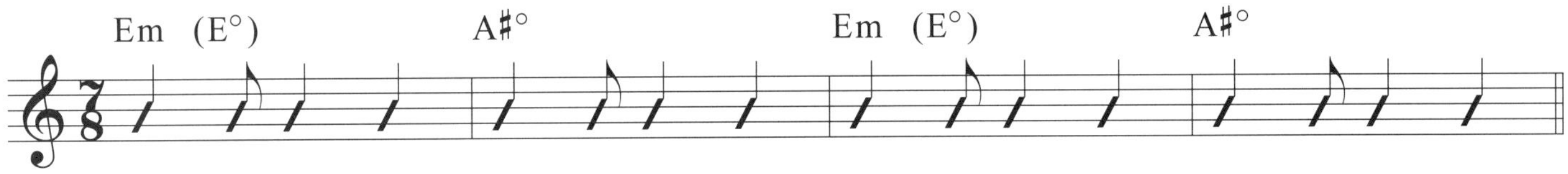

In other styles, like this Kato, we find a more modal chord progression.

Example 9

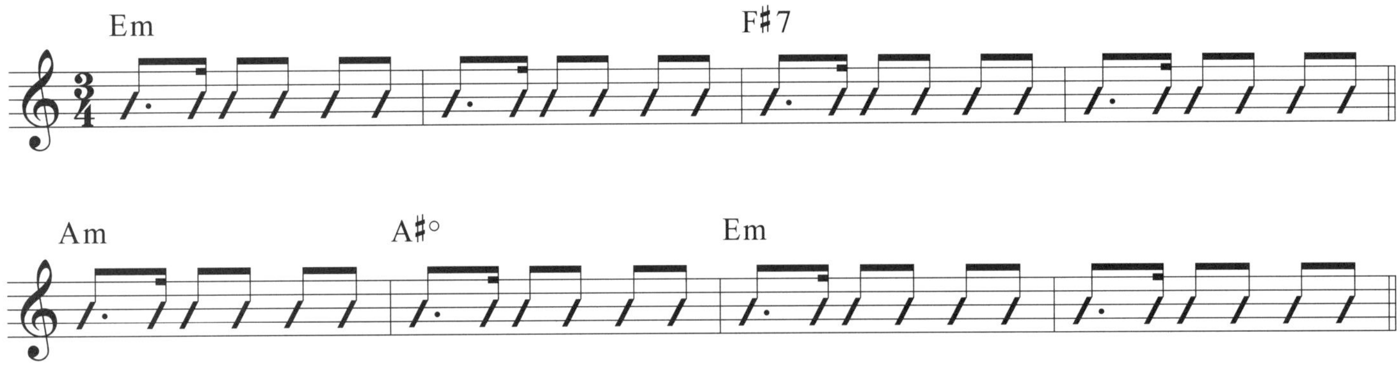

Here is a tonal (major scale-based) chord progression found in a Hasaposerviko style.

Example 10

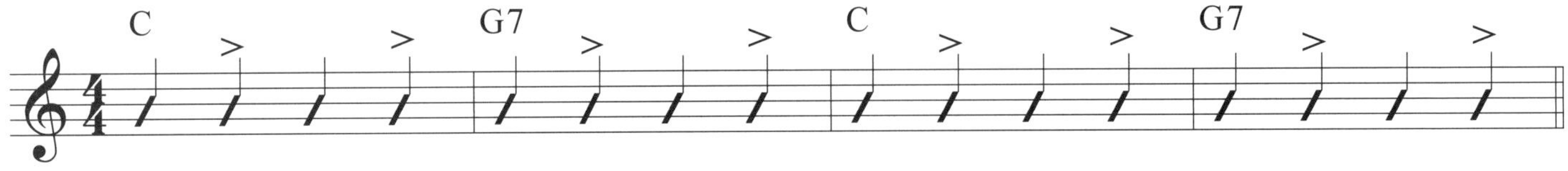

GREEK RHYTHMS

Rhythms in Greece are a constant party. For a musician from the West who has little experience with odd meters, Greek music will serve as excellent practice in this regard. We find odd meters like 5/8, 7/8, or 9/4, and even a simple 3/4 Tsamiko or 6/4 Tsikisto rhythm can become a lot of fun when we learn its typical performing patterns.

Many rhythms in Greek music have a cyclical character. This approach to rhythm is to be found all over the Eastern world, from India to Eastern Europe. The good news is the closer we get to the West, the less developed they are. So it becomes easier to learn and internalize them.

Here are a few rhythm patterns written down in a simple way to help you understand their basic feel.

Hasapikos Rhythm

Example 11

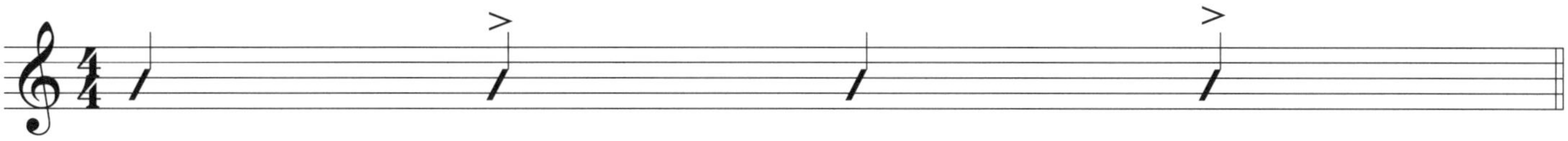

Kalamatianos Rhythm

Example 12

Karsilamas Rhythm

Example 13

Tsamikos Rhythm

Example 14

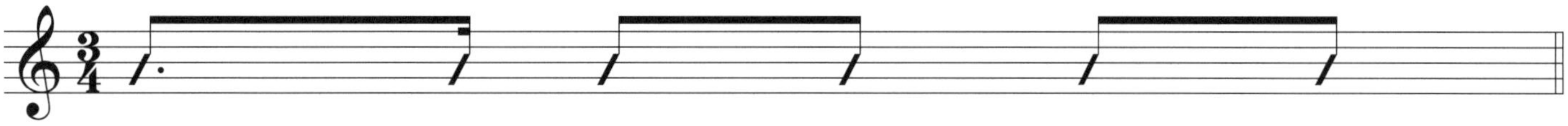

Tsikistos Rhythm

Example 15

Zeybekikos Rhythm Pattern 1

Example 16

Zeybekikos Rhythm Pattern 2

Example 17

Tsifteteli Rhythm

Example 18

Dactylos Rhythm

Example 19

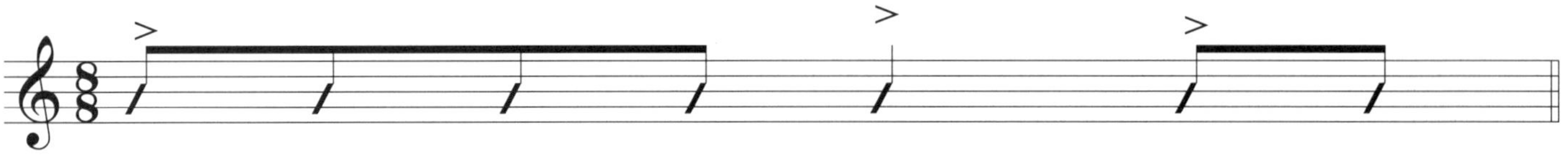

WORKING WITH THE VIDEO RECORDING

In this book, we have included videos complementing the information written in these pages. Please do not make the mistake of using only the book or only the video, because you will miss much valuable learning information.

In the video, you can watch the real performance of every piece of music followed by a brief explanation of certain details. Following is a slow tempo performance for you to see right- and left-hand details. You can also use this slow performance as practice to play along to before you are ready to try the actual tempo.

Be aware that, in some cases, the slow versions do not contain the repeats. Therefore, you'll need to refer to the score and/or the real performance version in order to play the original music structure.

ZEYBEKIKO

Zeybekiko is the name of a Greek music style belonging to what is called Rebetiko music. Rebetiko is also known as the "Greek blues" because of the similarities in the lifestyle of the bluesmen in North America and the Rebetiko musicians. Many Greeks living in Turkish lands were shifted back to Greece and forced to leave all their belongings. They arrived at the city to discover that the government didn't have resources to help them. Left with nothing, many tried to make a living playing music. Many Rebetiko songs talk about the tough life they were bearing.

Zeybekiko comes from Zeibeks, who were a lineage of warriors found in Anatolia. Hence, we find the Zeibekiko rhythms in both Greece and Turkey. But you must remember that, although the beat count is the same, the rhythm performance differs in both places.

More than a style, we could say Greek Zeybekiko is mainly a rhythm because, melodic or harmonically speaking, it doesn't differ much from other styles inside of Greece. It's based on a count of nine beats with a characteristic rhythmic pattern:

Example 20

This same pattern can be started from different points in a cyclical way. This can only occur in different tunes, however, meaning that you cannot break this cycle within the same tune. So one song might have one starting point of the pattern, and a different song could have another starting point, etc. In the next example, you can see the previous pattern starting on the fourth beat (this fourth beat now becomes the first).

Example 21

In the following tune, we will use the first pattern. It is very important that you practice this pattern in a simple way first. You can take one chord and strum the pattern while tapping it with your foot. The idea is that, when you play the tune with its full arrangement, you can be tapping the Zeybekiko rhythm with your foot. This practice will help you feel the style's groove and sound more genuine.

Example 22

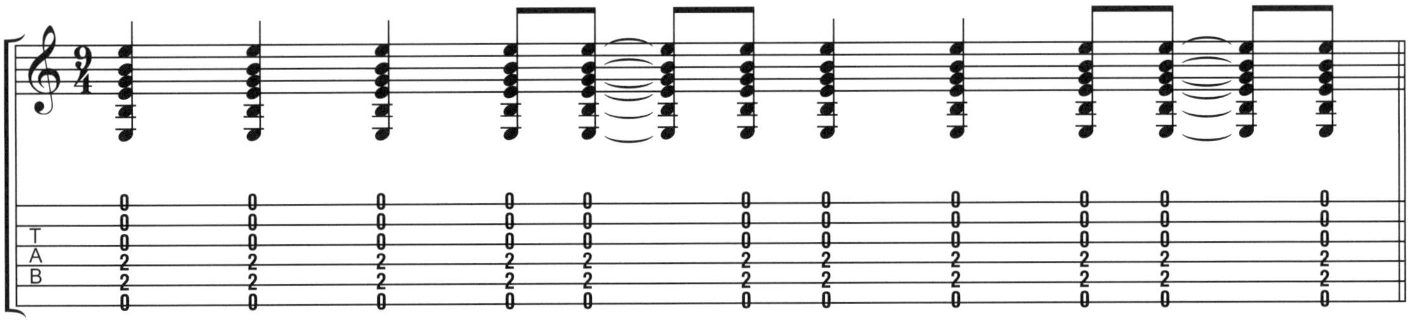

The melody in this tune is based on the E Dorian ♯4 scale we saw earlier in the book. Try to practice it well before playing the piece, as this will make learning the melody easier. You can also use this scale to improvise over the tune.

Zeybekiko

Composed by Fernando Pérez

INTRO

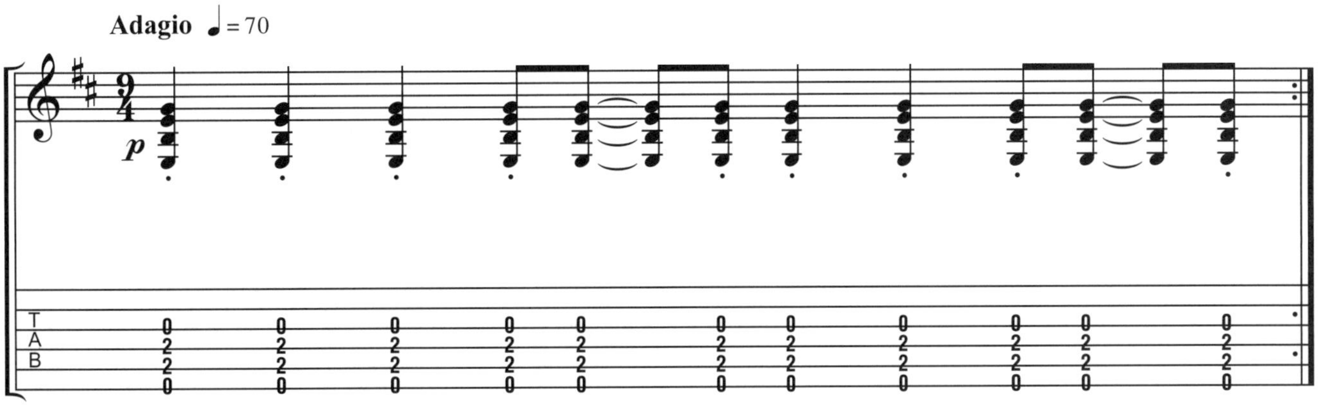

A

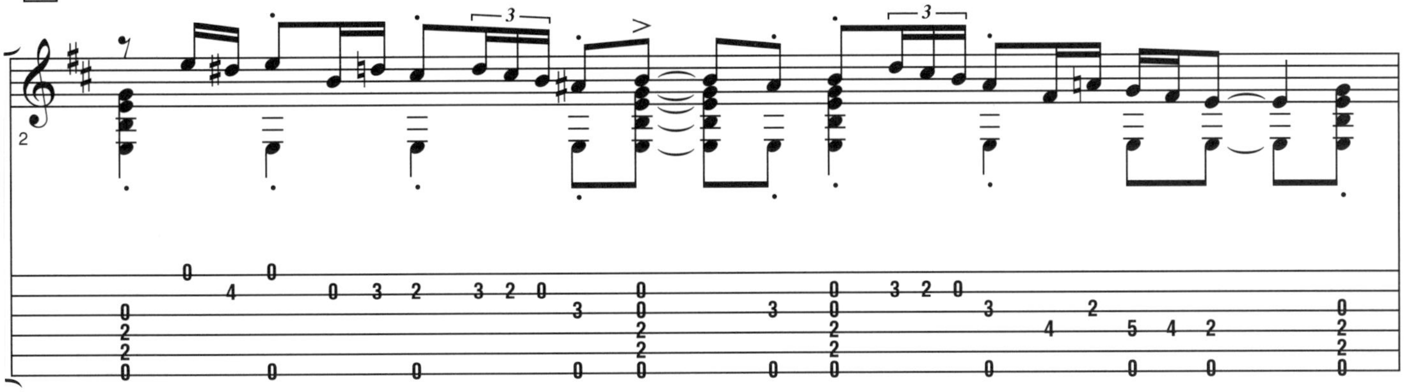

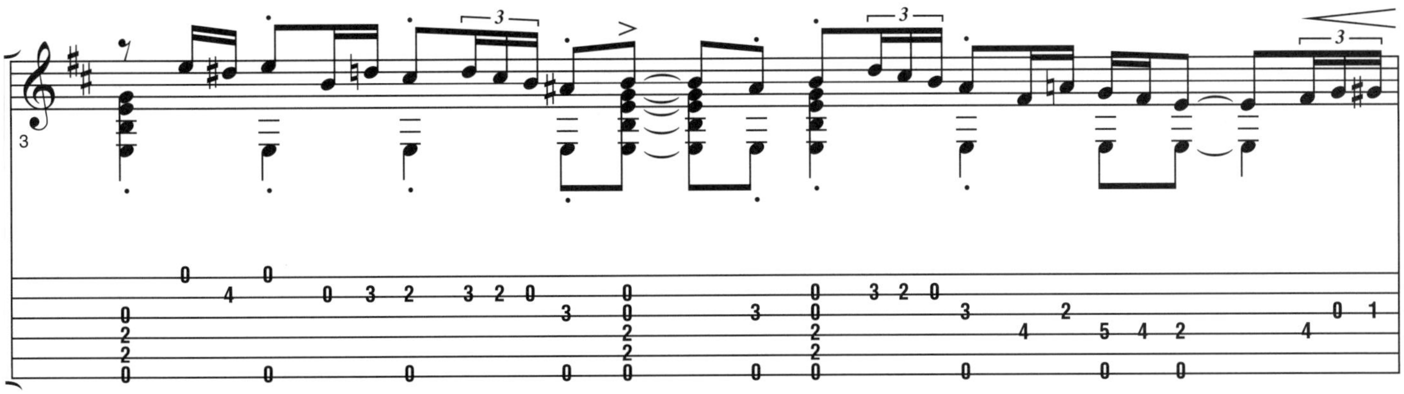

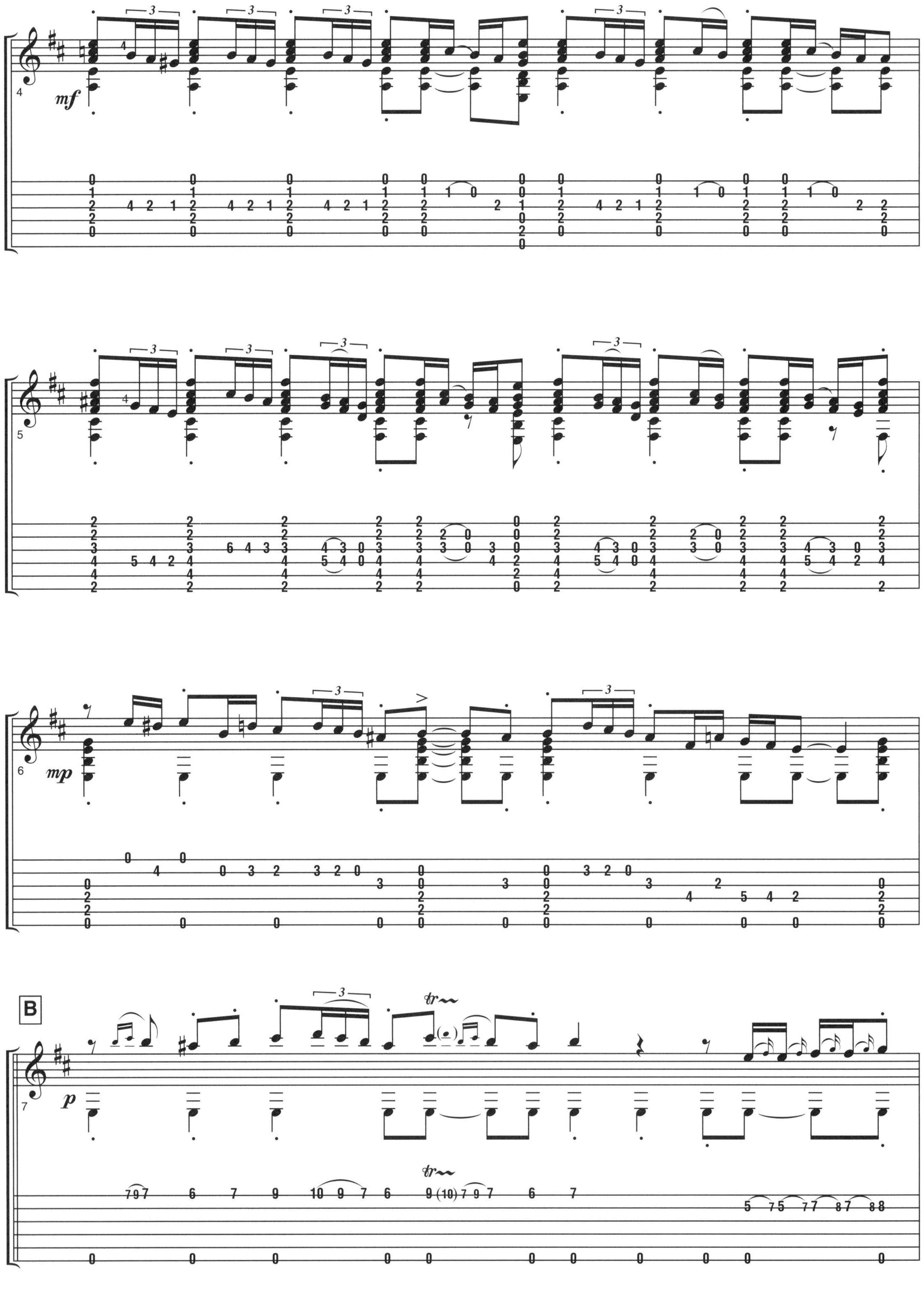
B

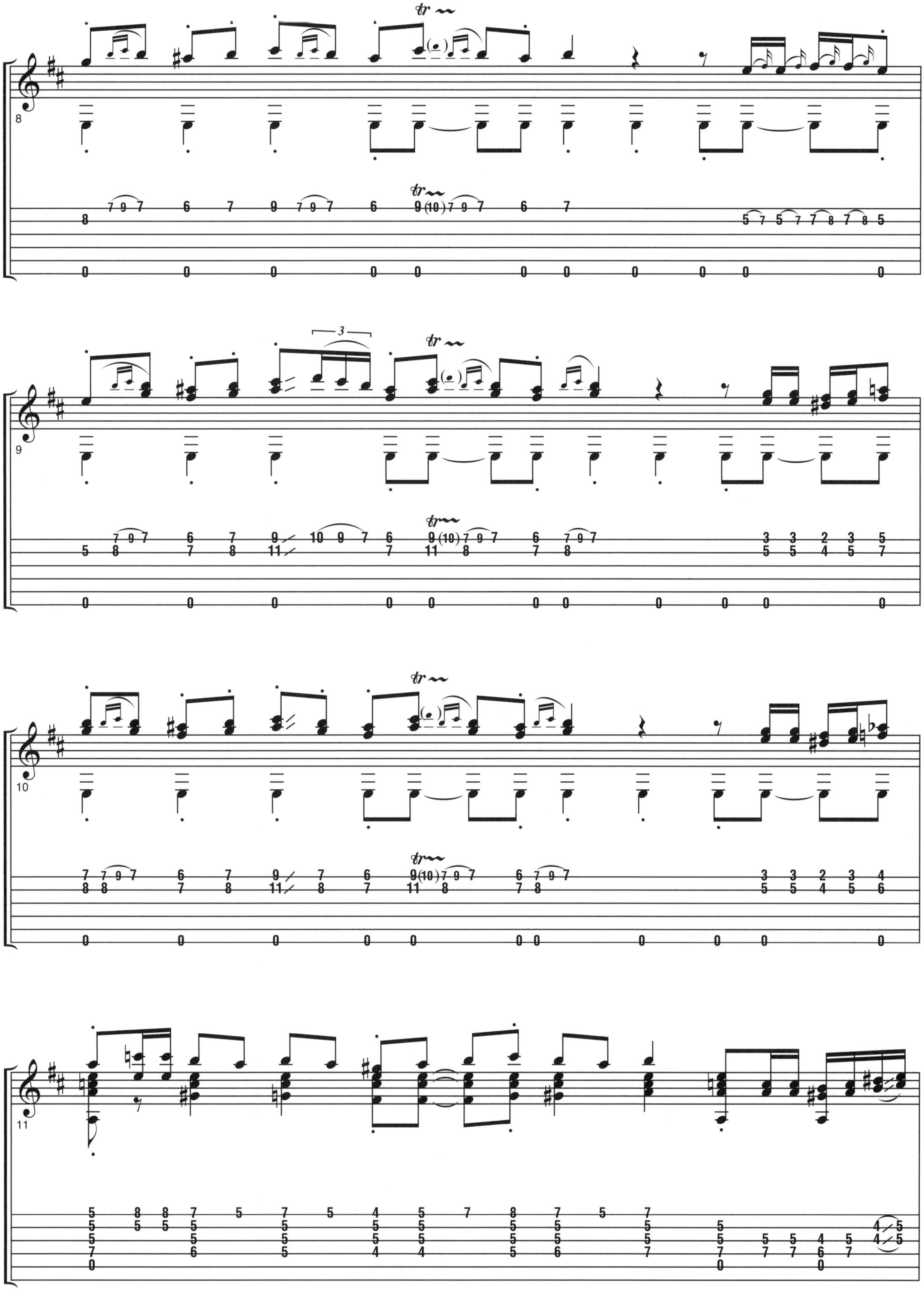
8
tr
9
3
tr
10
tr
11

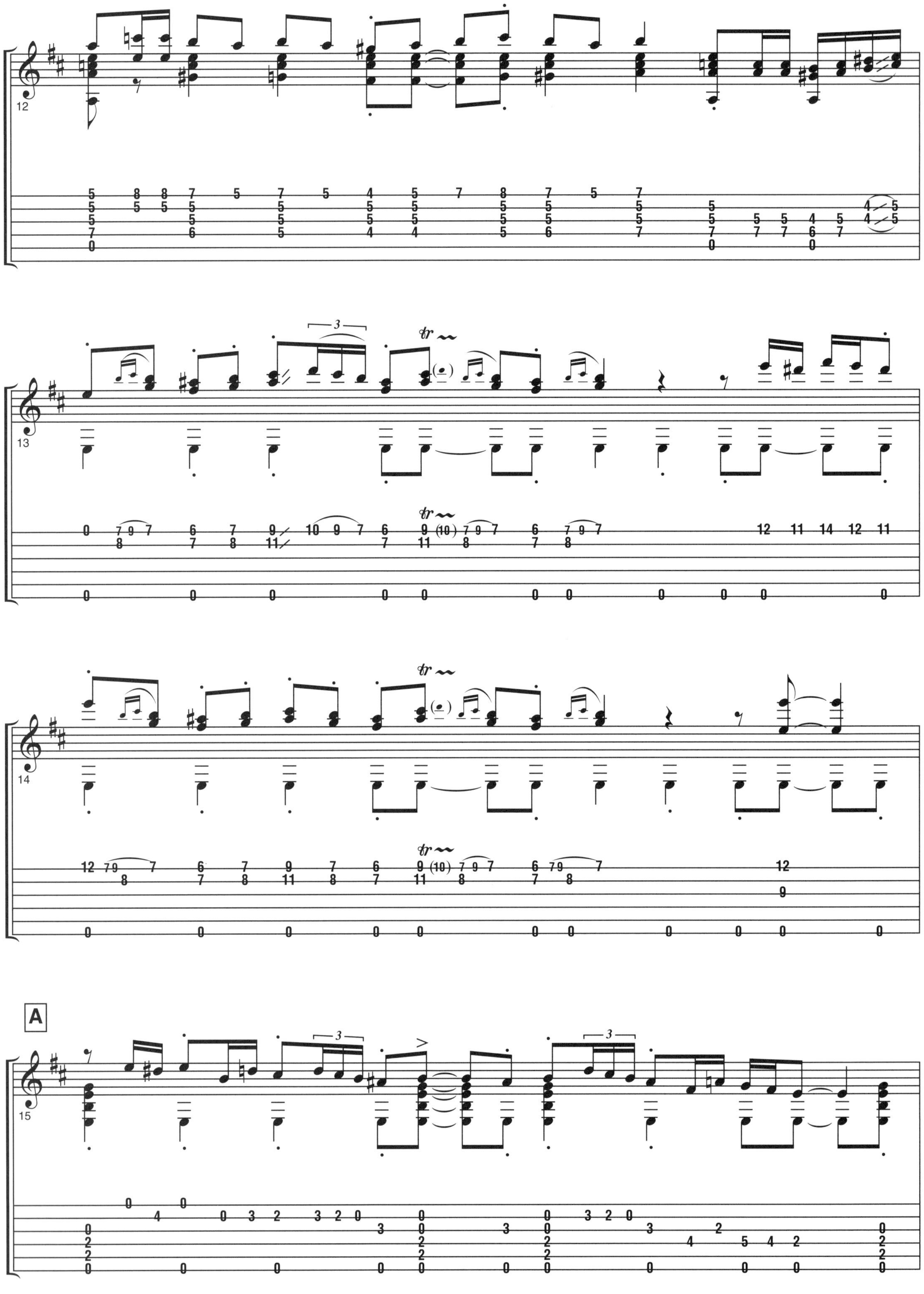
12
13
tr
14
tr
A
15

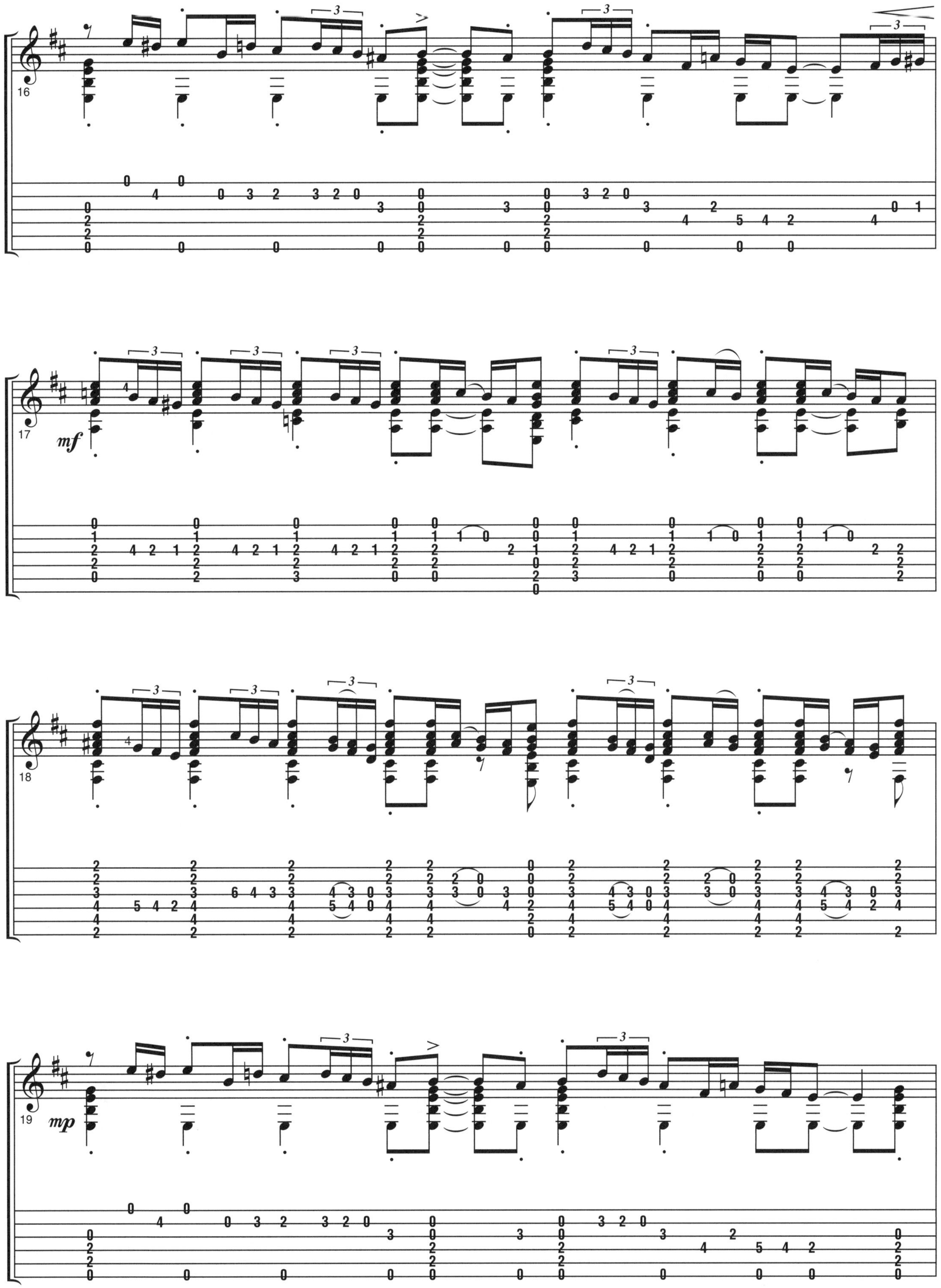
16
17
mf
18
19
mp

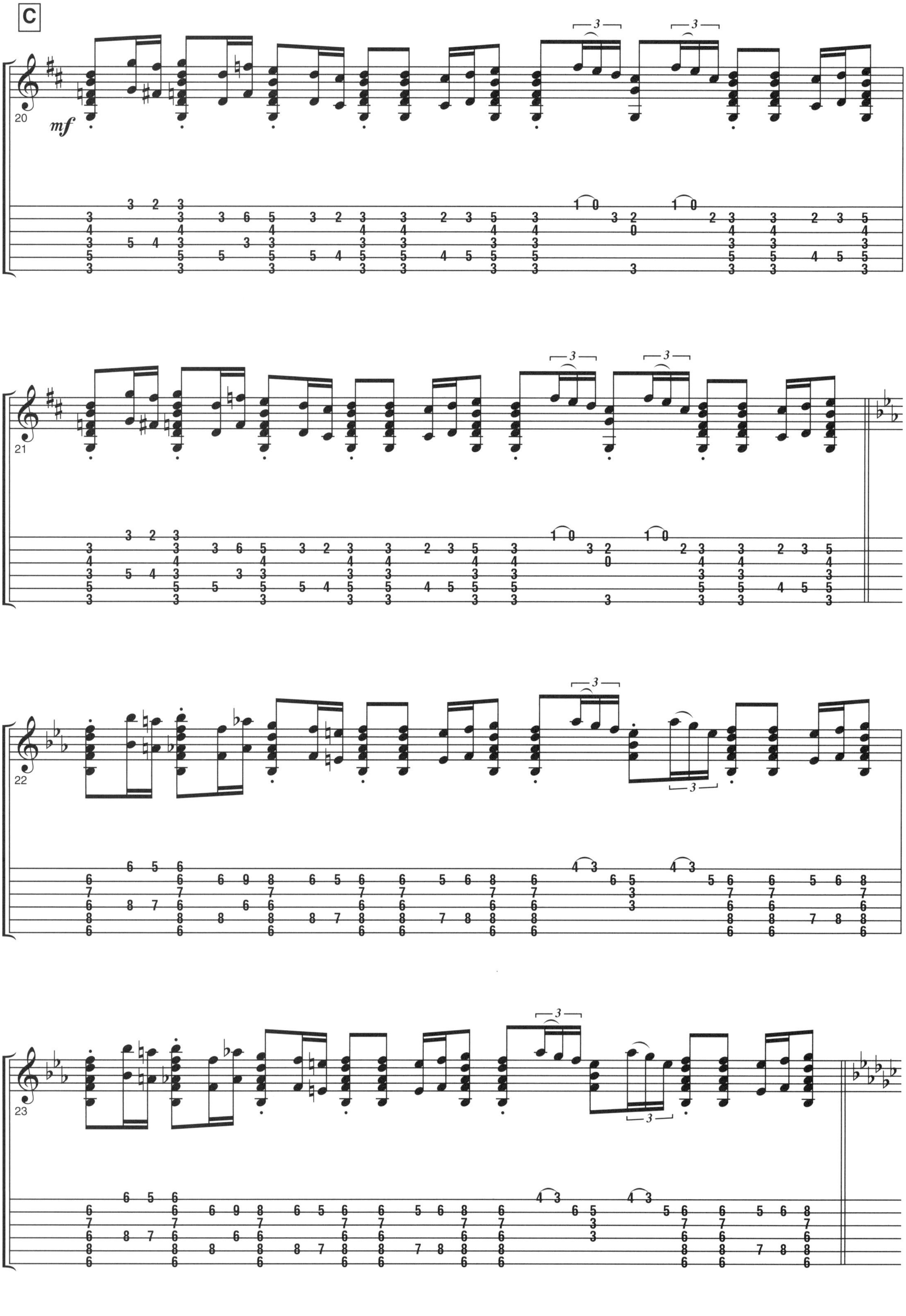
C
mf

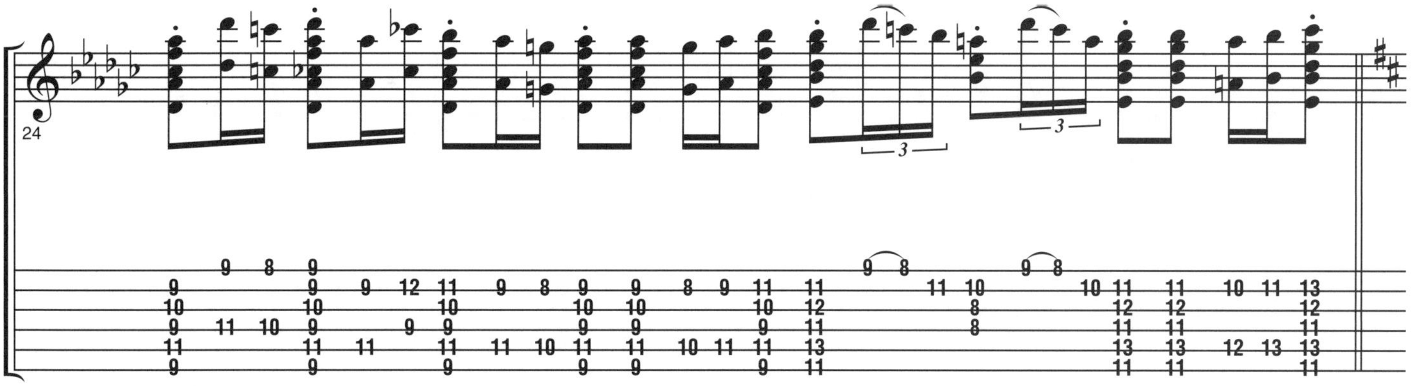

A Variation

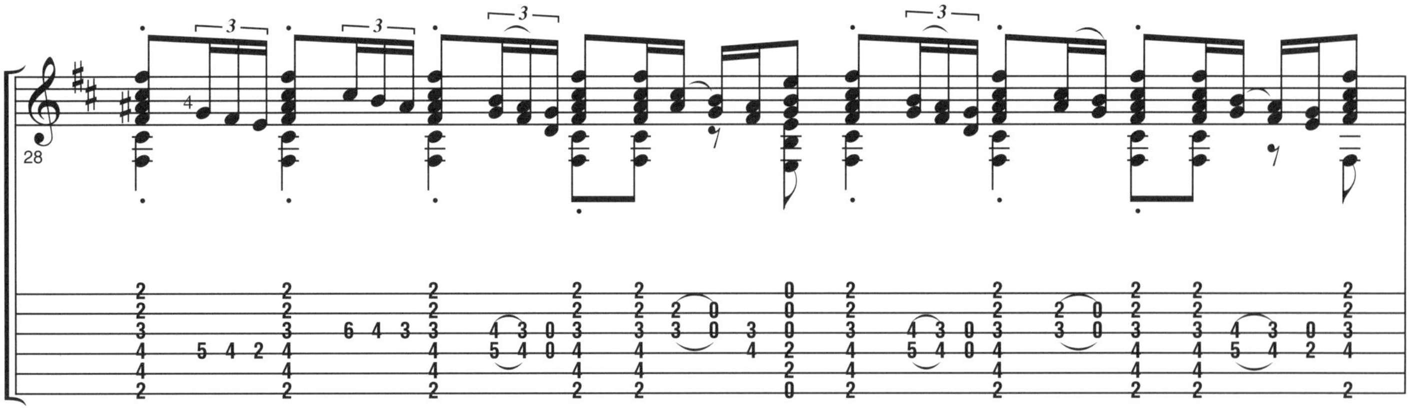

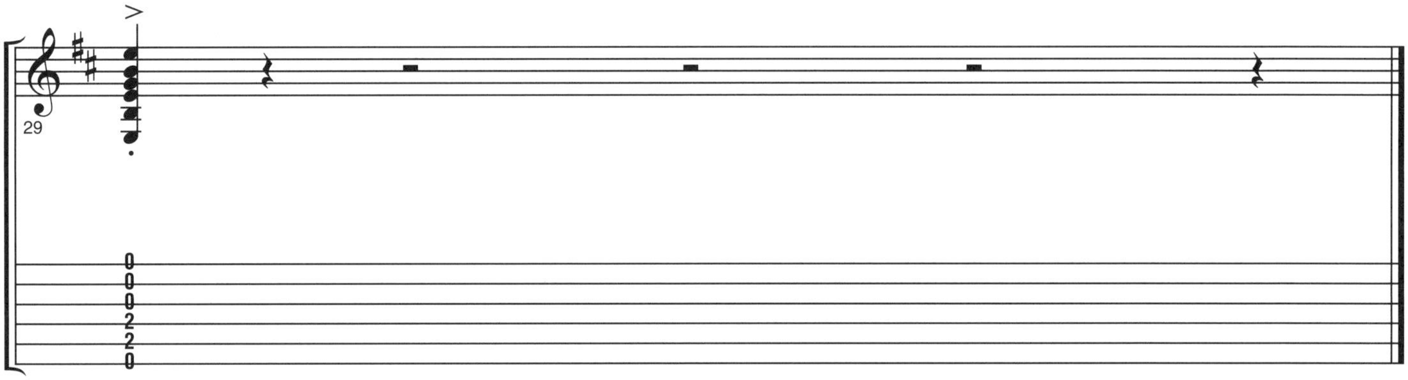

SYRTAKI

Syrtaki is a composition based in the Hasapiko style—a folk dance known as the "butcher's dance." It has two main versions: slow and fast. Here is where the famous Syrtaki style (which gives name to this tune) comes from. Syrtaki, which is not a real Greek folk dance, was created as a combination of both types of Hasapiko. So it is a Hasapiko starting slow and finishing fast.

The melodies, along with their harmonies, are based in a minor key. The rhythm is a bouncing 4/4 time. Pay attention to the recording to see how the tempo fluctuates and even stops in certain moments. It is very important that you give some mystery to the melody.

Syrtaki

Composed by Fernando Pérez

INTRO

Andante ♩ = 100

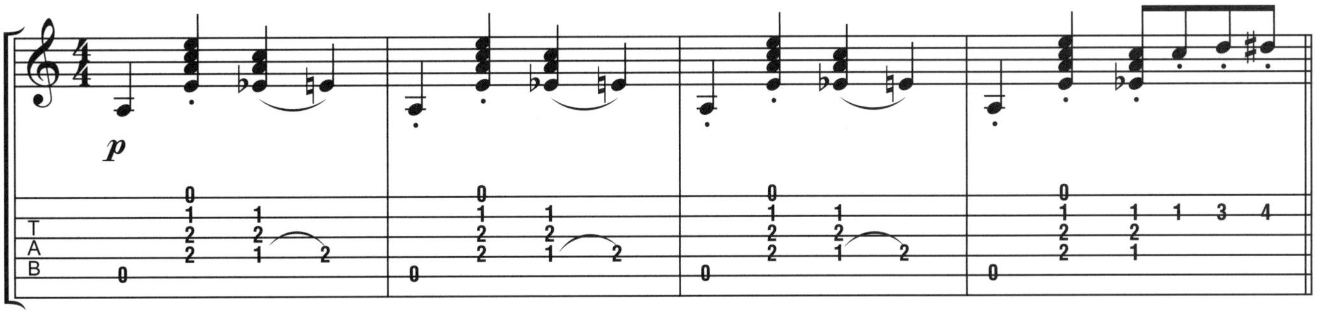

A

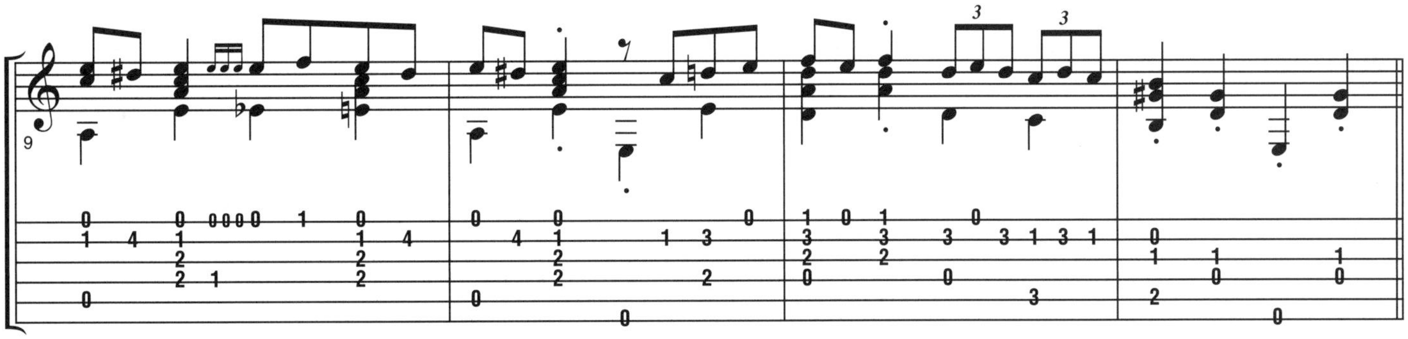

B

C
accel.
mf
deccel.

INTRO

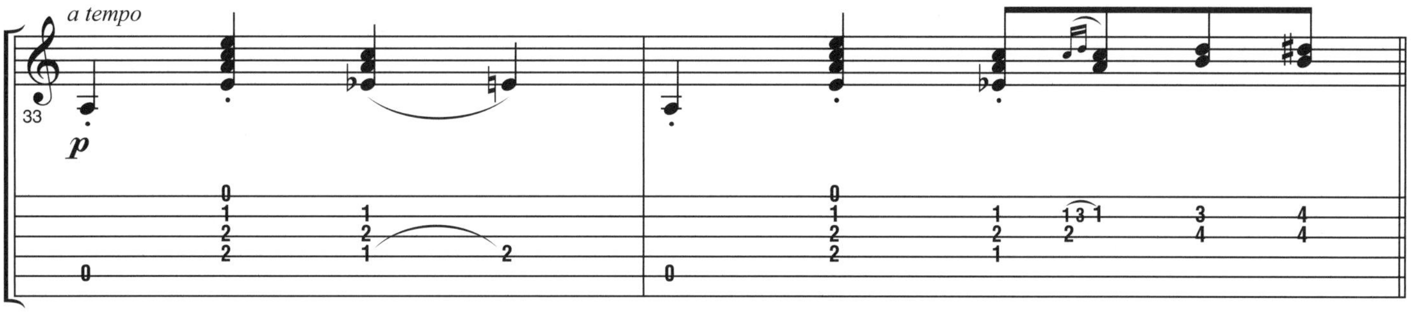

A Harmonized

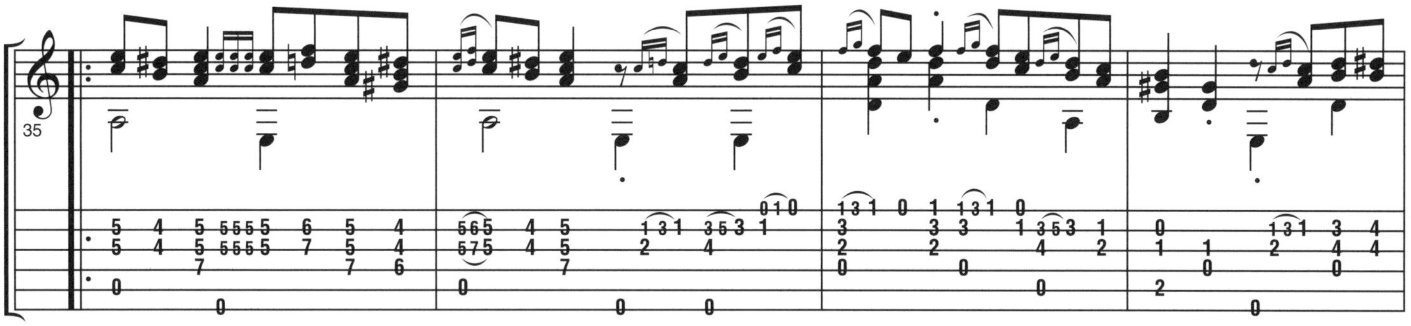

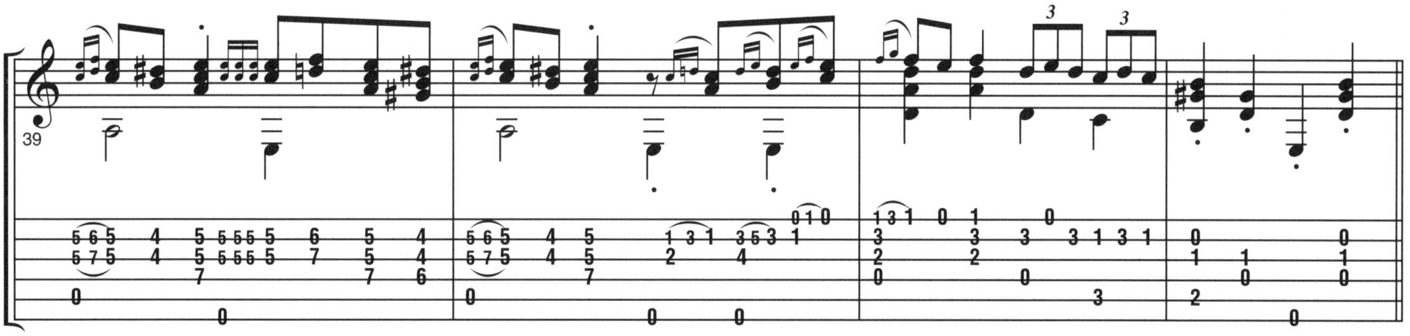

B Harmonized

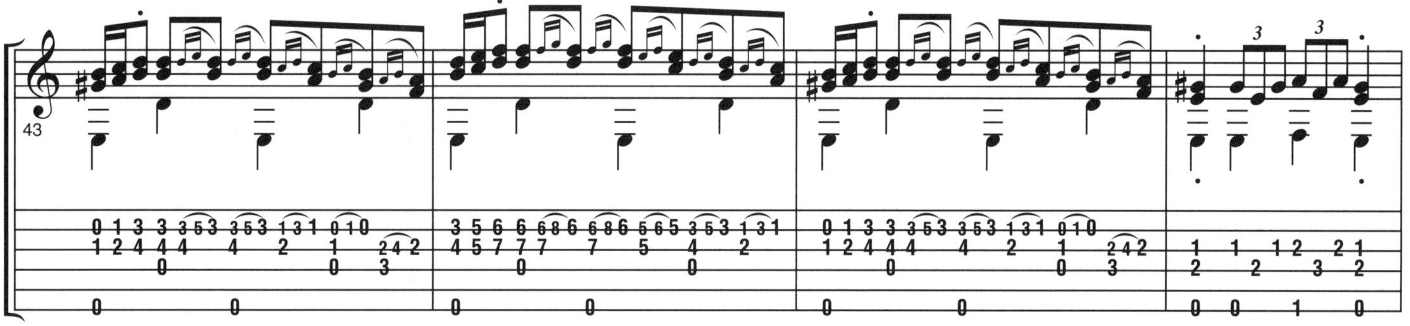

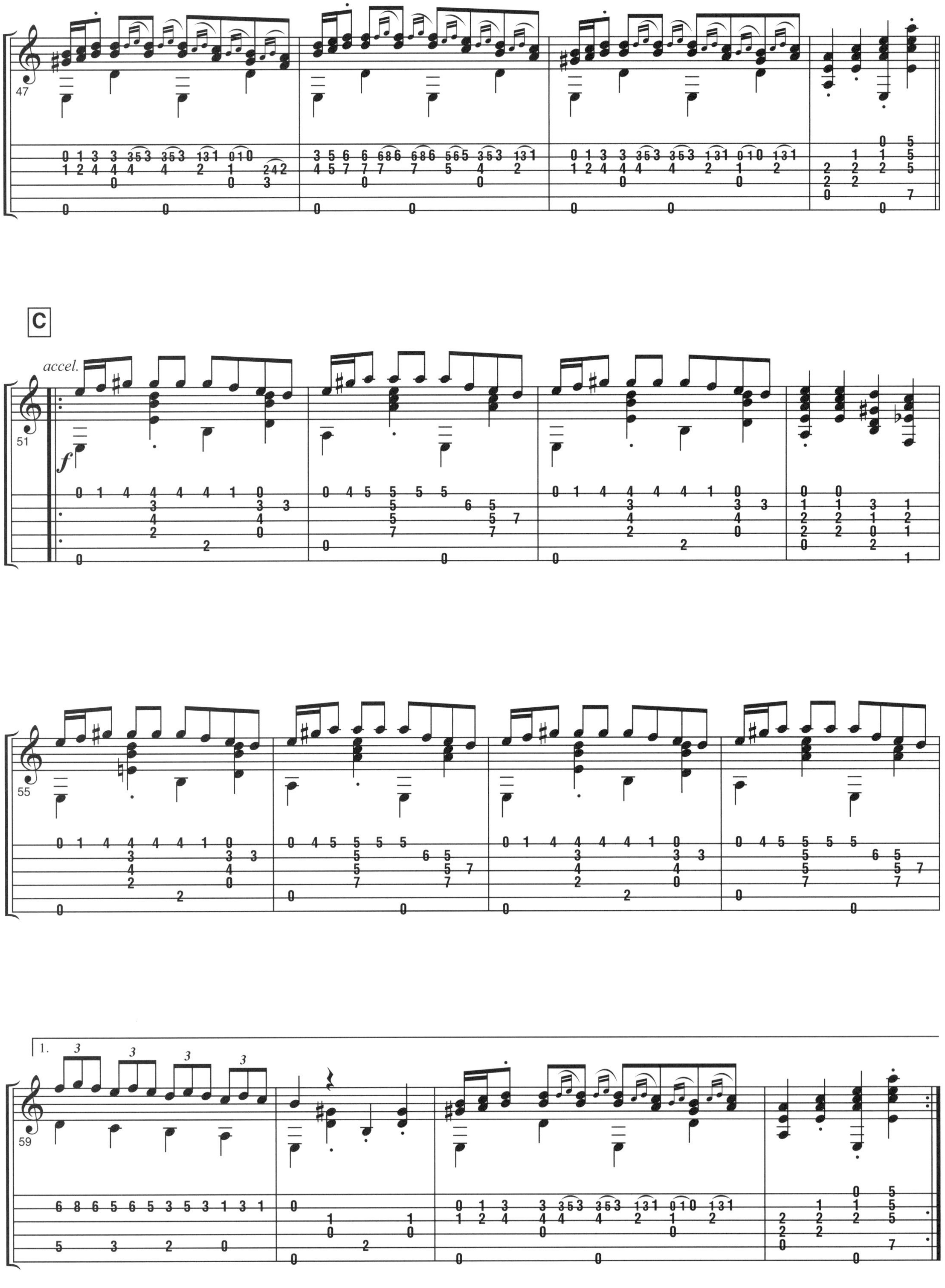
C
accel.
f
1.

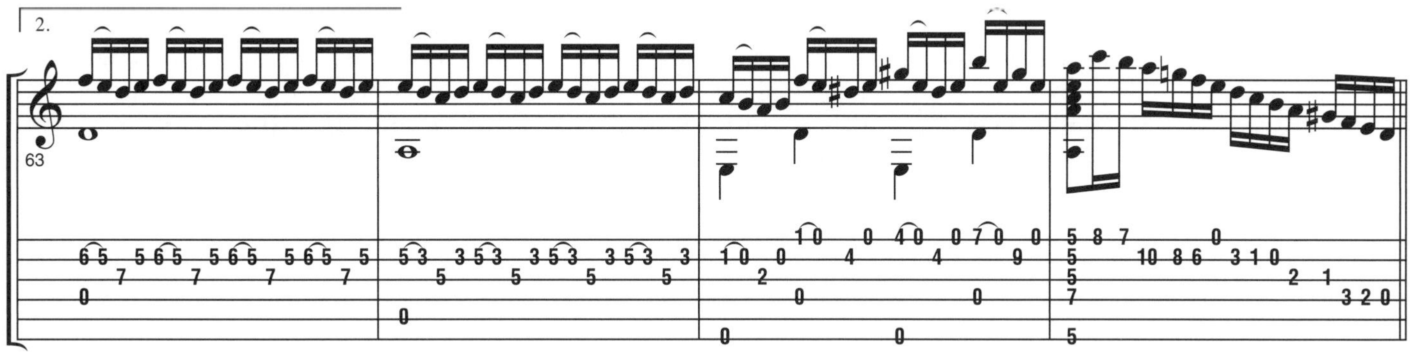

C Double Time

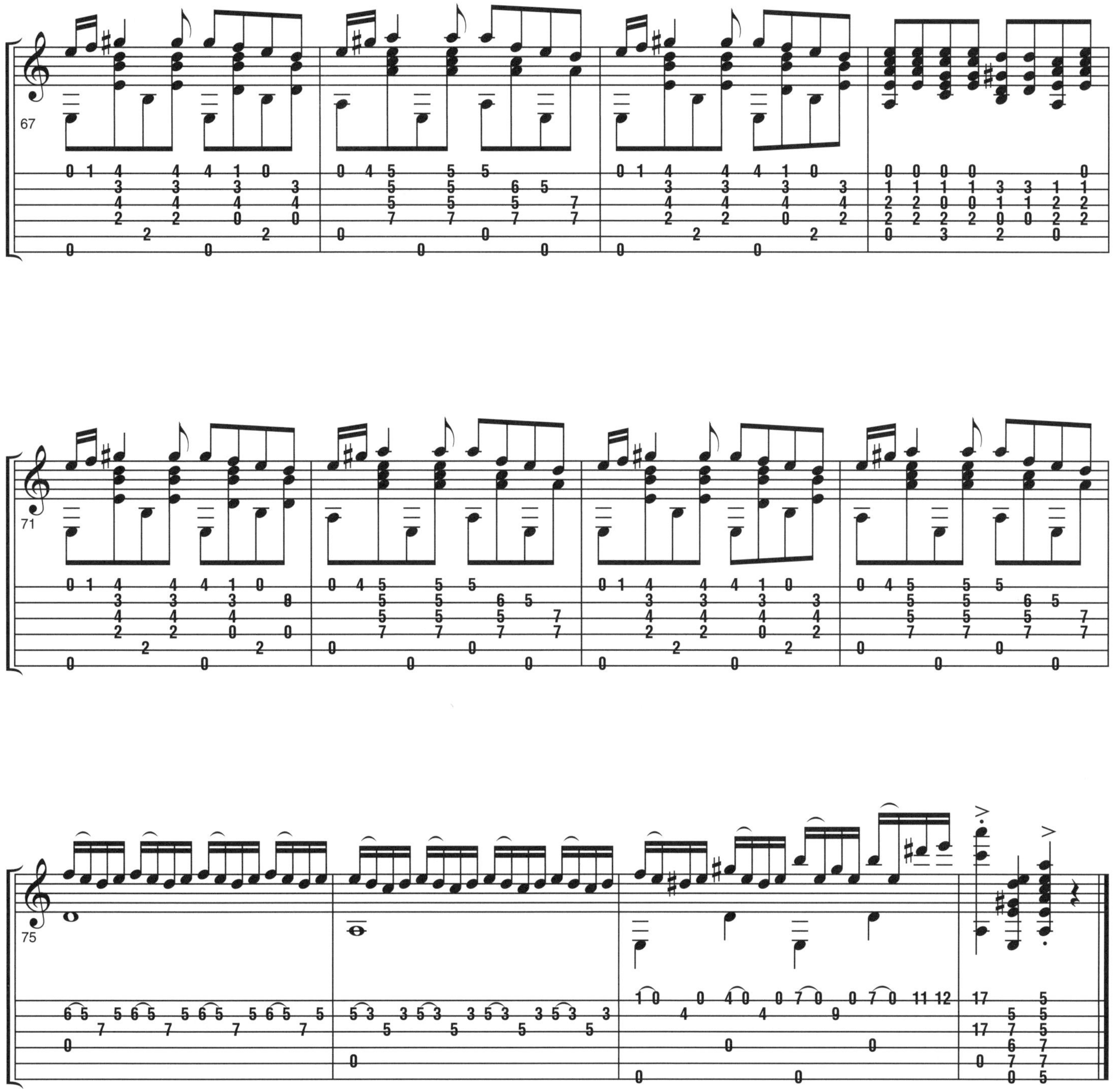

KARSILAMAS

Karsilamas is originally a folk dance. We find it in Greece as well as Turkey because it has been spread across Asia Minor. The name is Turkish and means something like "face to face salutation." In Greece, we find Karsilamas and another similar dance called Antikrystos meaning basically the same thing "face to face". The rhythm is in 9/8 with a subdivision of 2+2+2+3:

Example 23

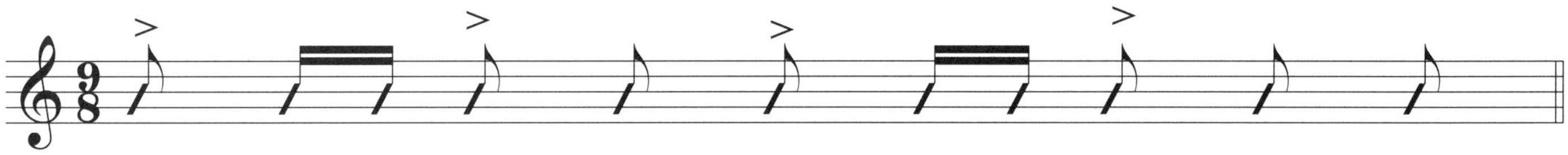

Here is a Karsilamas especially composed for guitar. There is a main part that alternates with other variations. Again, practice the rhythm first by strumming only one chord and keeping the beat count with your foot. You can tap your foot as if it was a 4/4, making the fourth beat last longer.

Karsilamas

Composed by Fernando Pérez

INTRO

Allegro ♪ = 250

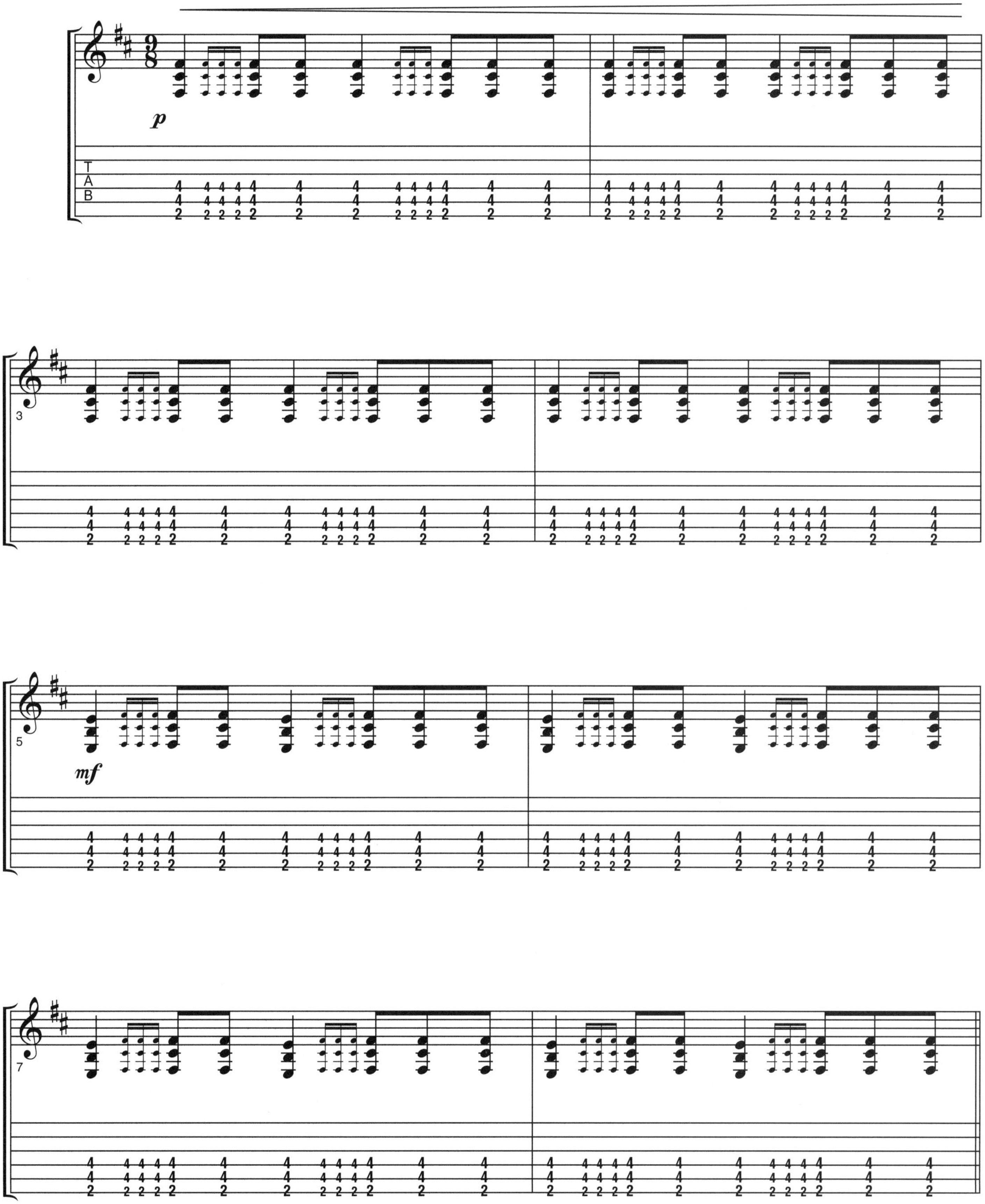

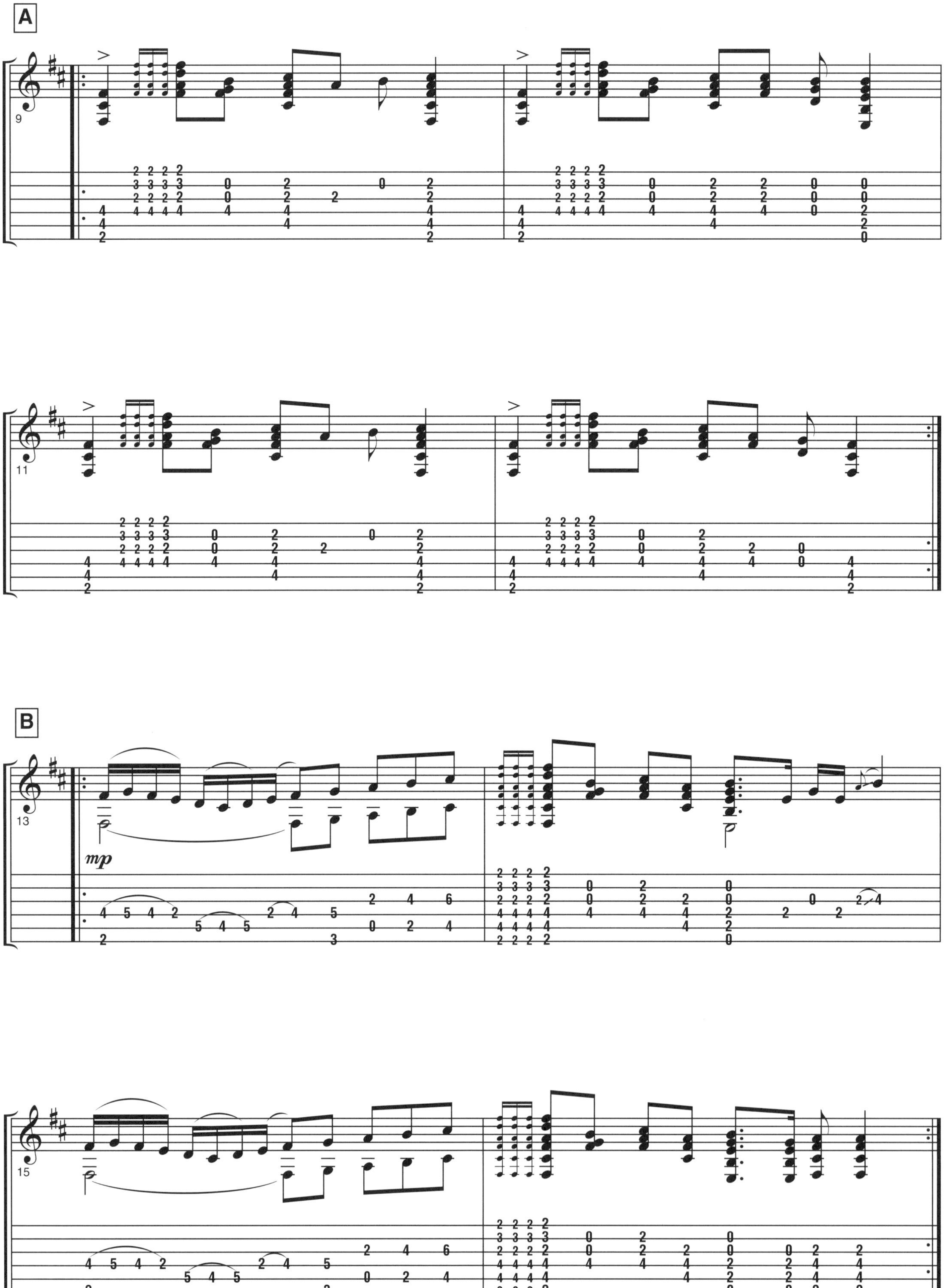
A
9
11
B
13
mp
15

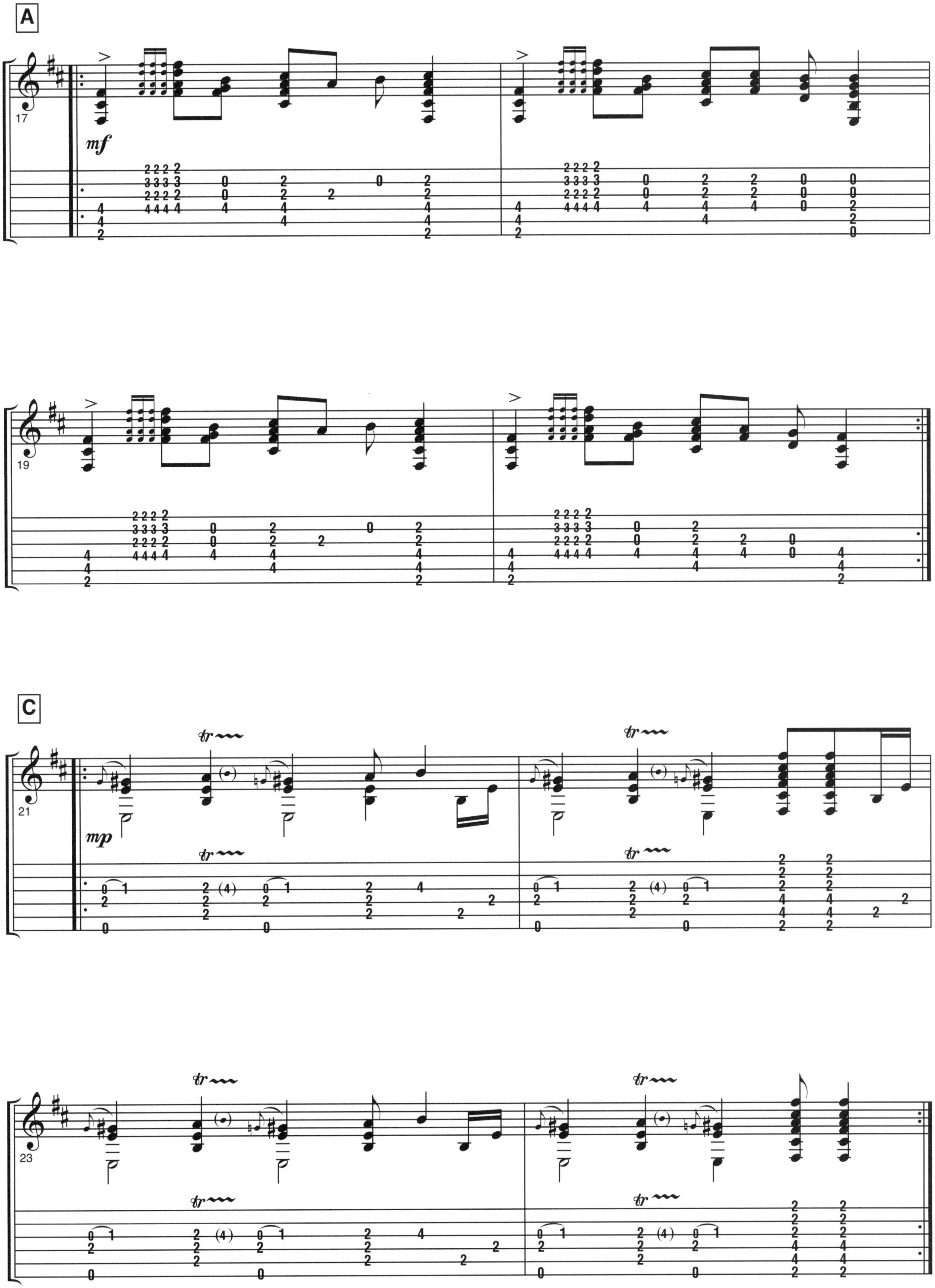
A
mf
C
mp

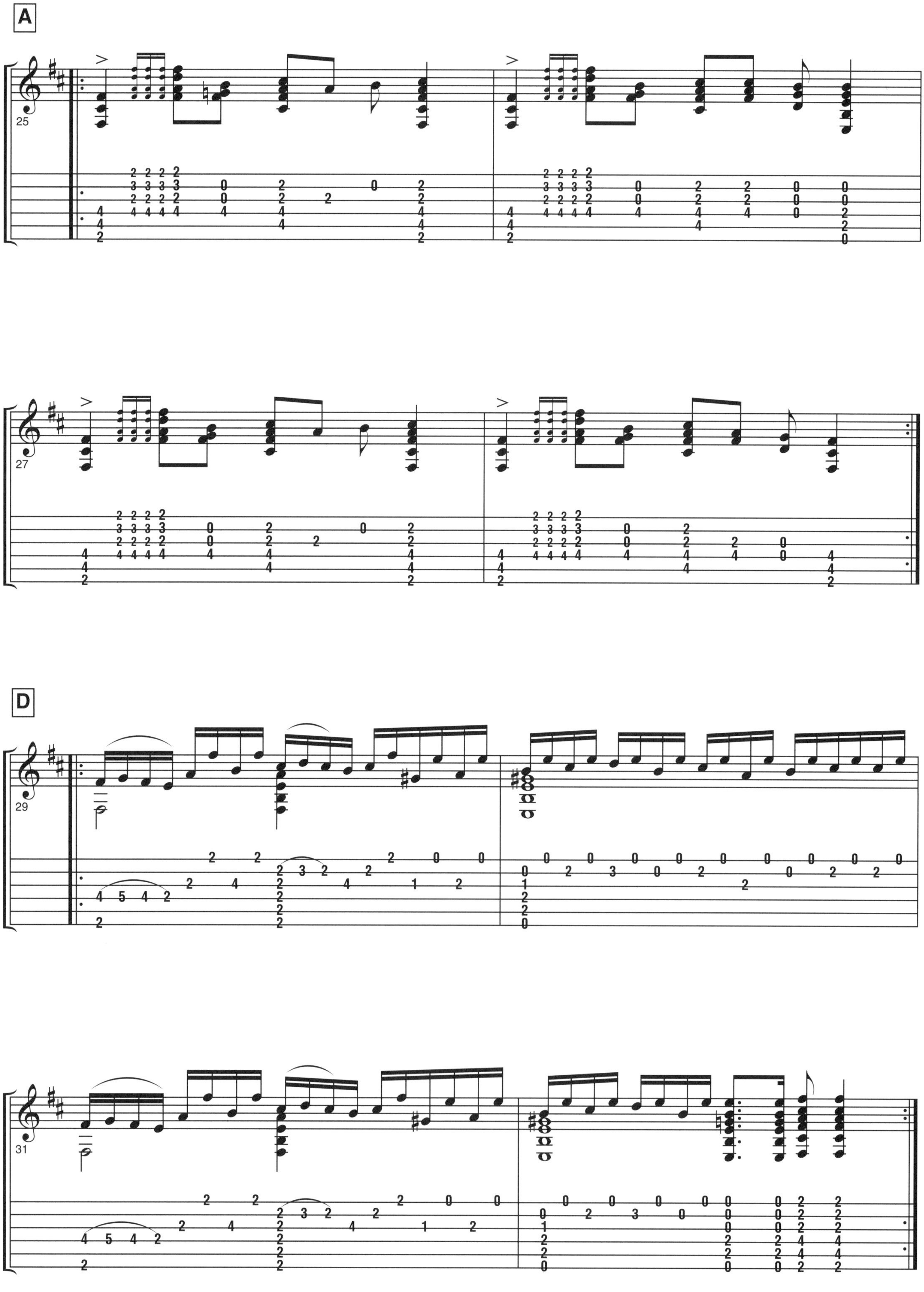
A
25
27
D
29
31

A Variation

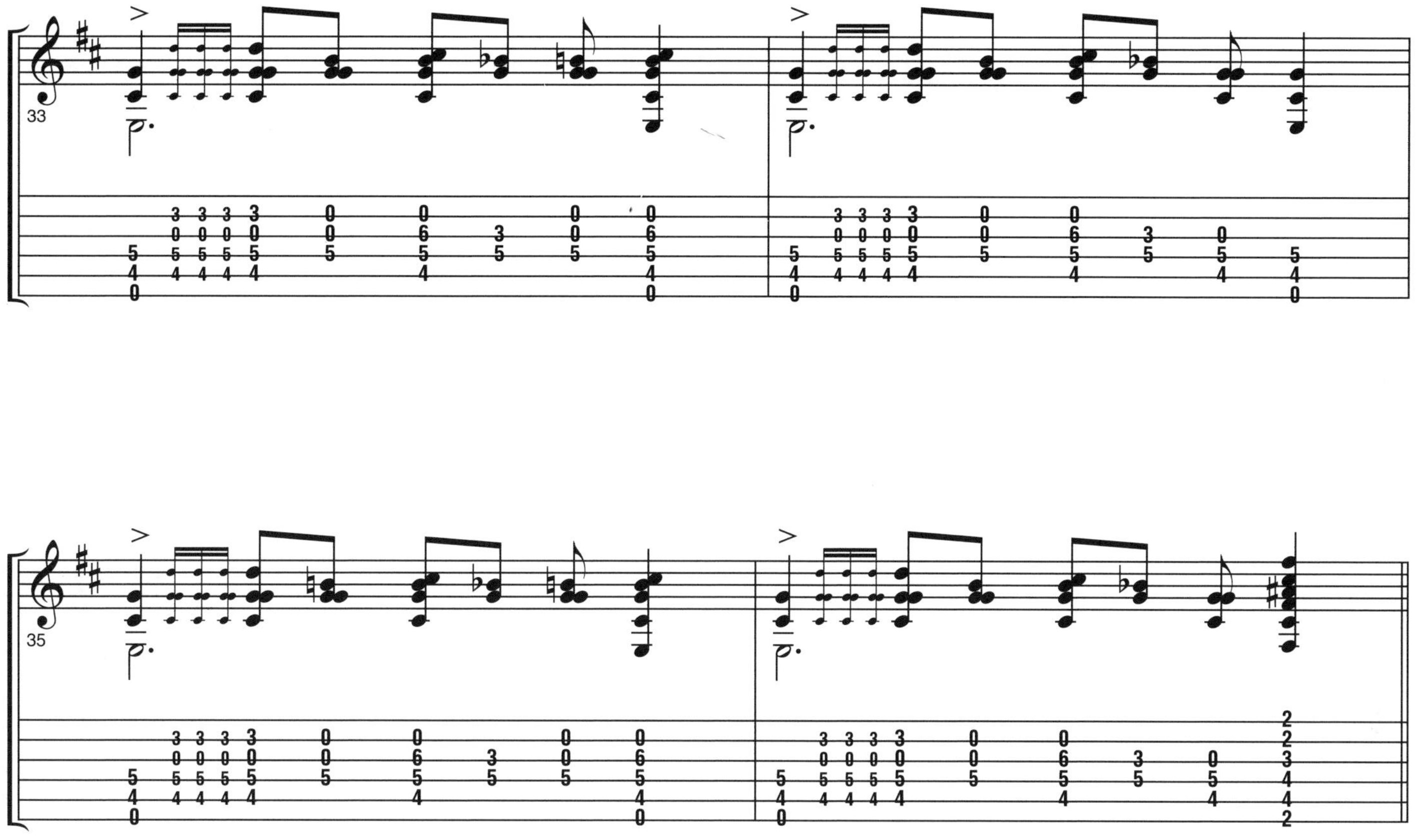

A

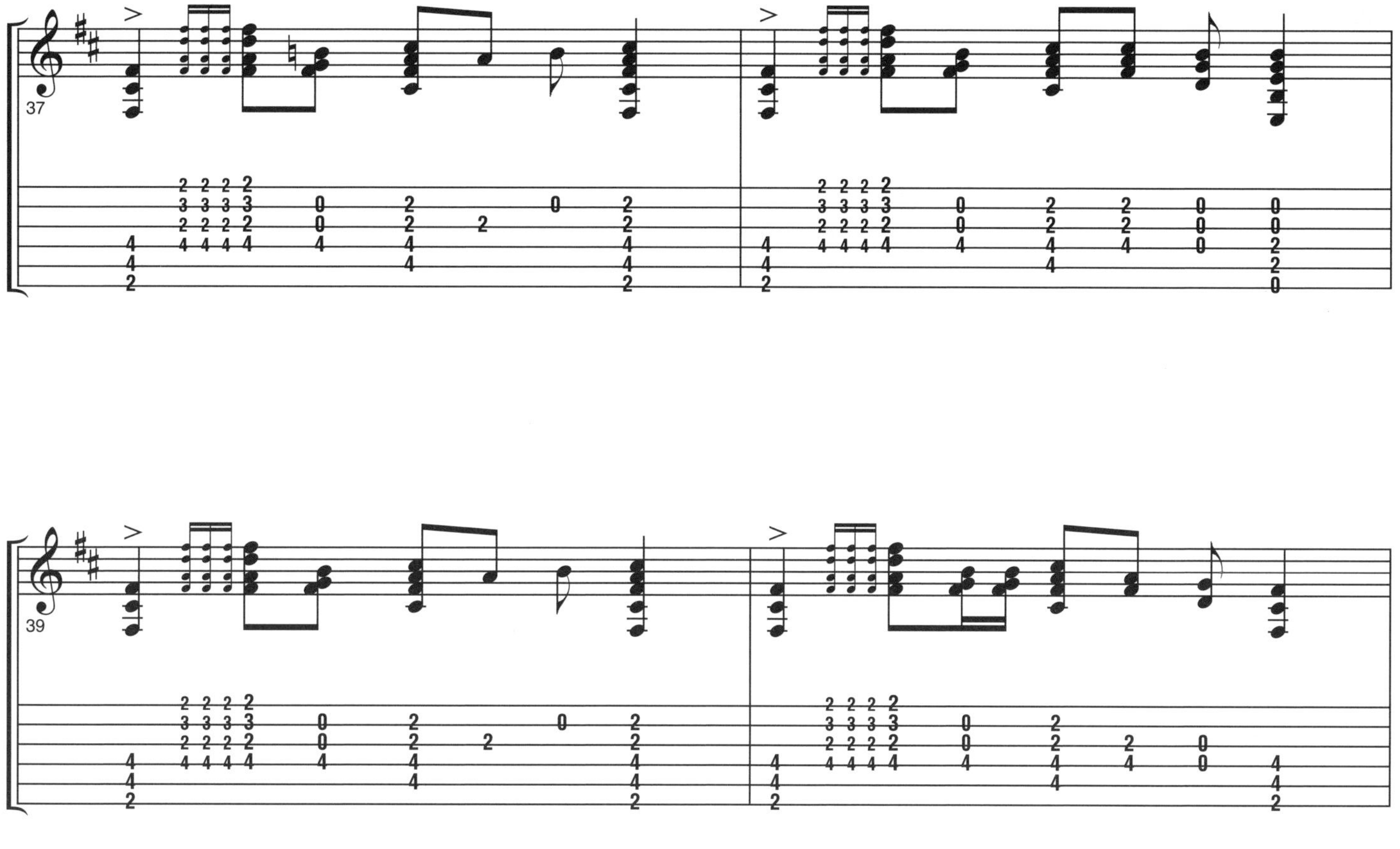

ENDING

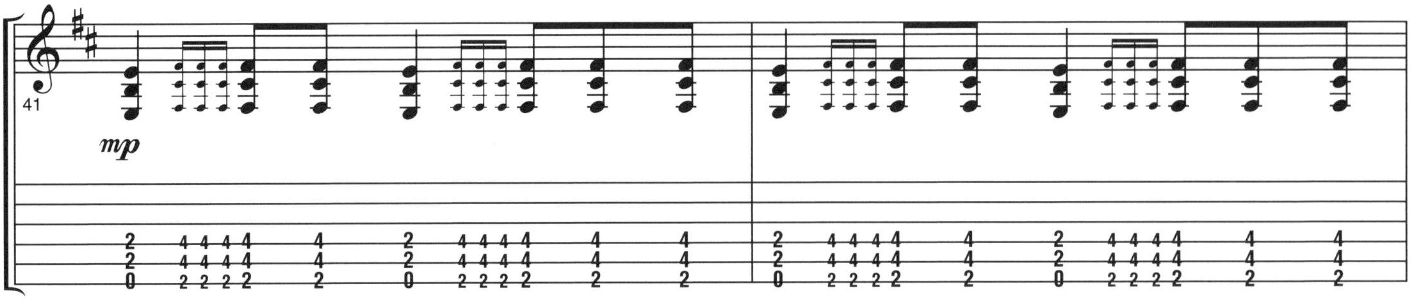

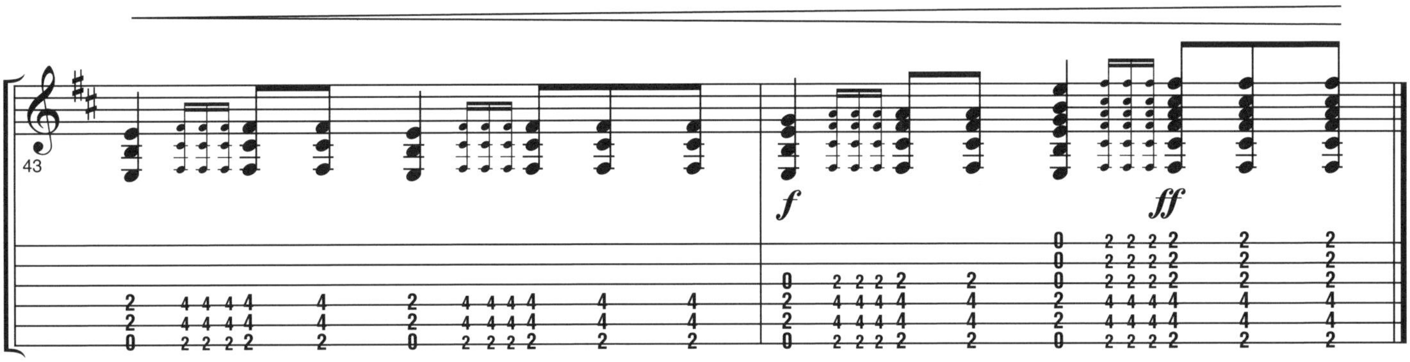

TSAMIKO

Tsamiko is also a traditional folk dance from central Greece. This tune has been composed especially for guitar and combines the Tsamiko rhythm with an air in the melody, which can be found all across the country, reaching the Balkans. The rhythmic pattern is very easy. It's written in 3/4, and all you have to do is pay attention to not speed up the tempo. This Tsamiko in particular needs to keep a heavy feel.

To play this tune, we'll put the capo on the third fret and read the notes as if we were not using the capo. The sixth string with the capo on would actually become G, but we'll consider it as an E for ease of reading. After you learn the tune, you will be able to place the capo anywhere you like (or remove it).

Tsamiko

Composed by Fernando Pérez

Capo III

INTRO

Andante ♩ = 104

A
14
18
1.
20
2.
B
22

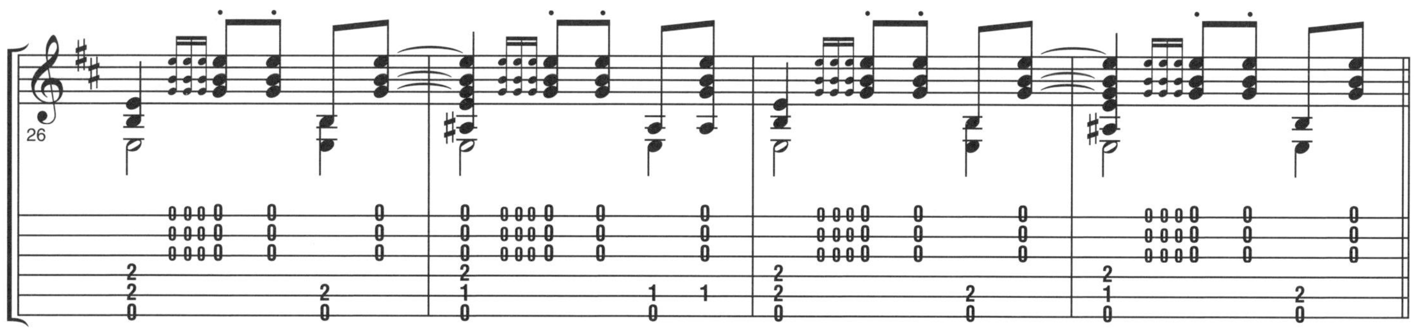

A Variation

B

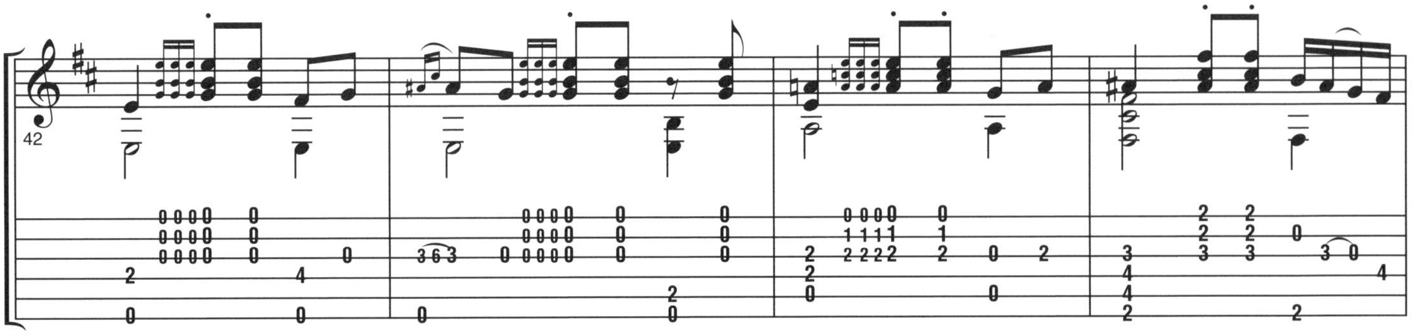

C

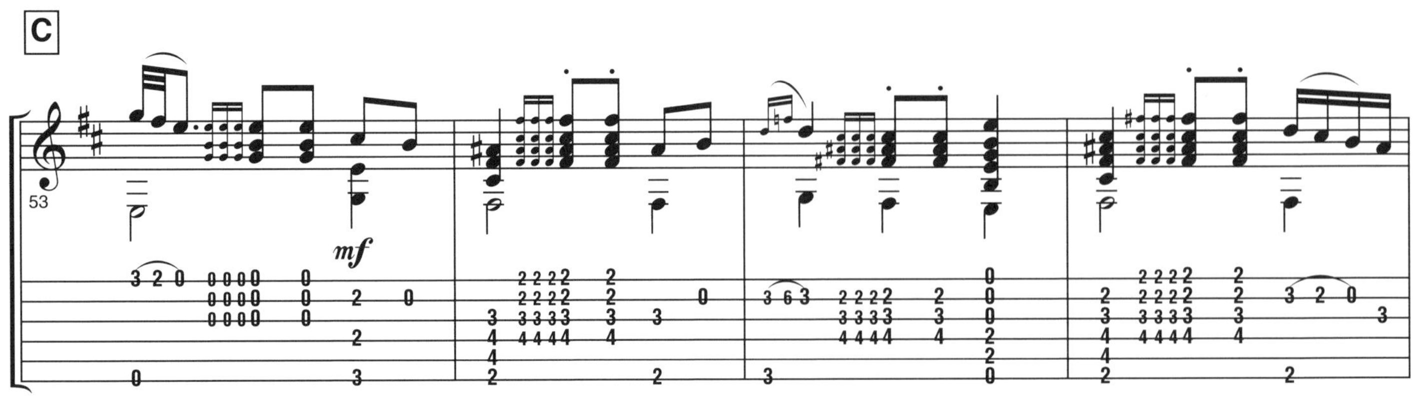

B **Variation**

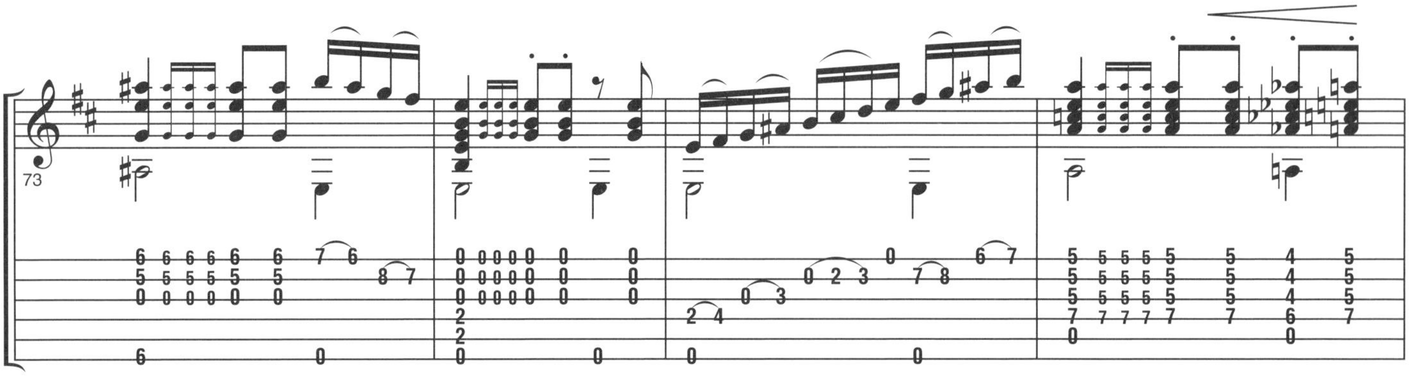

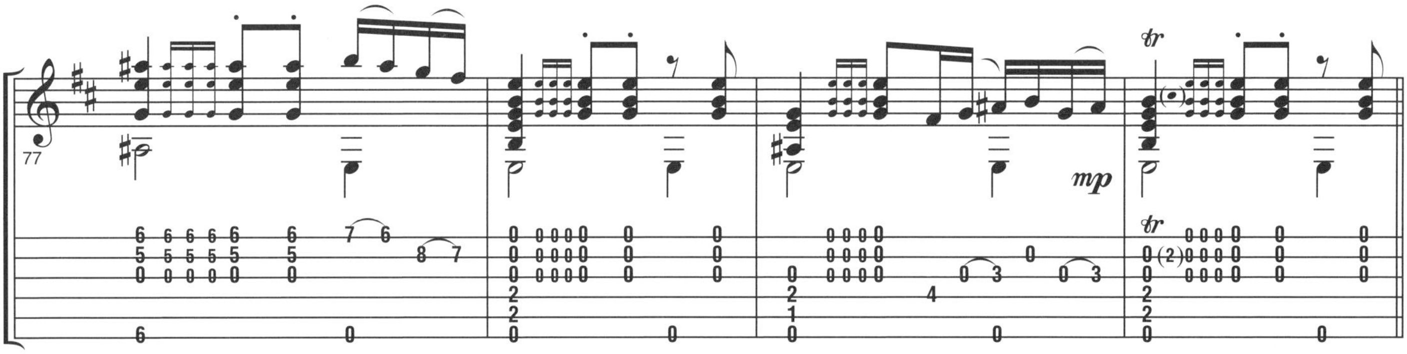

FINAL INTRO

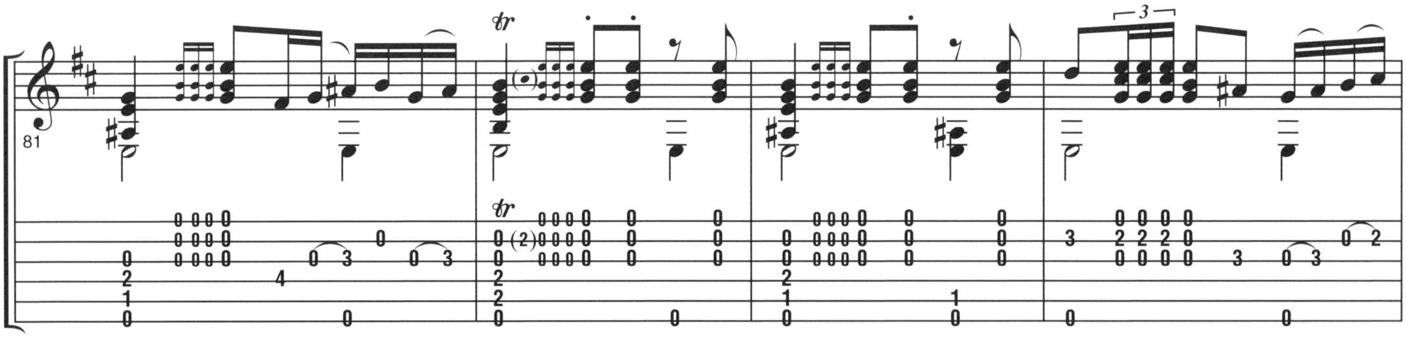

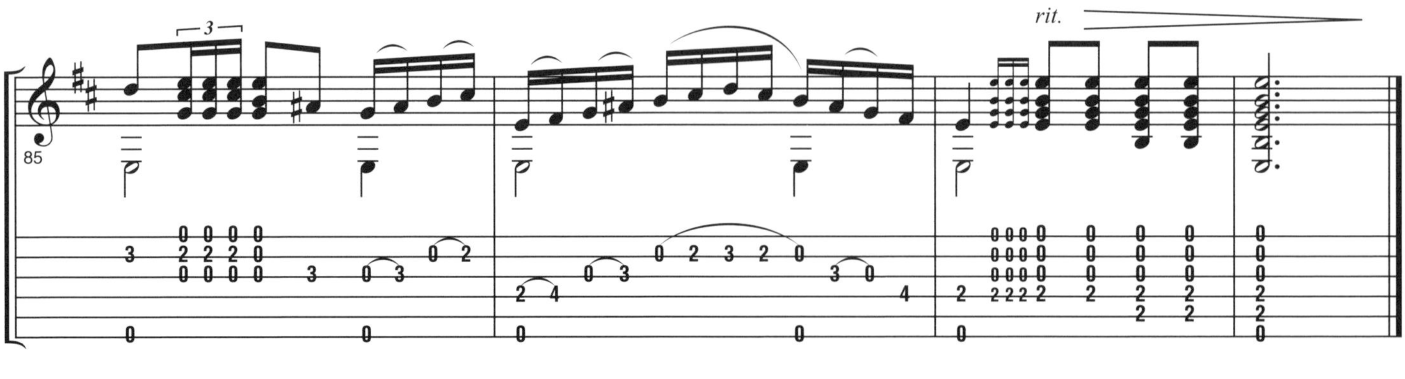

TO PAPOUTSI TON TSANKARI
(THE SHOEMAKER'S SHOE)
(Kalamatianos)

"The Shoemaker's Shoe" is a song based on the Kalamatianos rhythm. Kalamatianos comes from central Greece but is well known all over the country, as well as Cyprus and internationally. It is always cheerful and mainly used at parties and festivities.

The rhythm is in 7/8 and divided as 3+2+2. You should practice this time signature a little bit before you play the full guitar arrangement. Try saying the count division (3+2+2) out loud as you tap your foot on the first beat. You can also do this by strumming only one chord.

Example 24

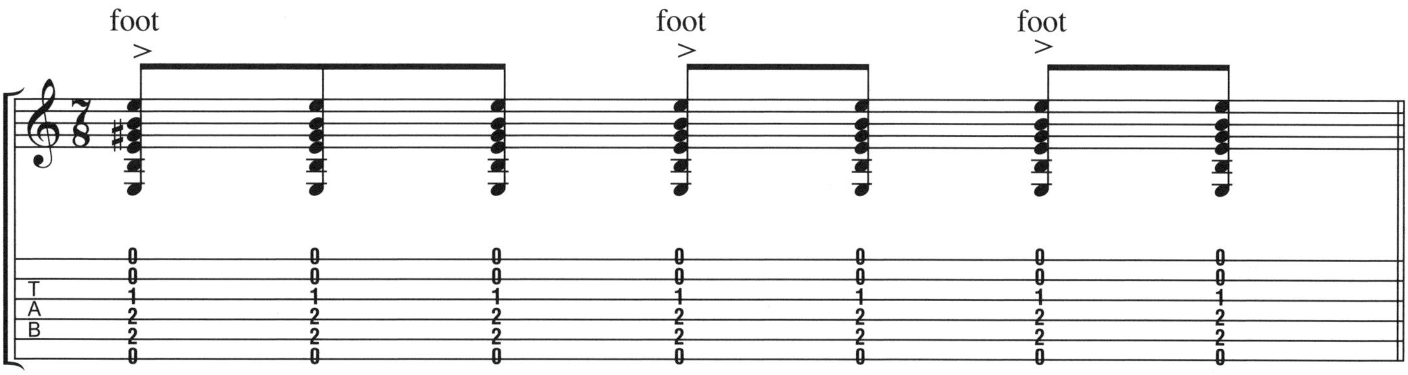

After this practice, you can start playing the tune, but always keep the accents very present with your foot.

To Papoutsi ton Tsankari

"The Shoemaker's Shoe" (Kalamatianos)

Composed by Fernando Pérez

INTRO

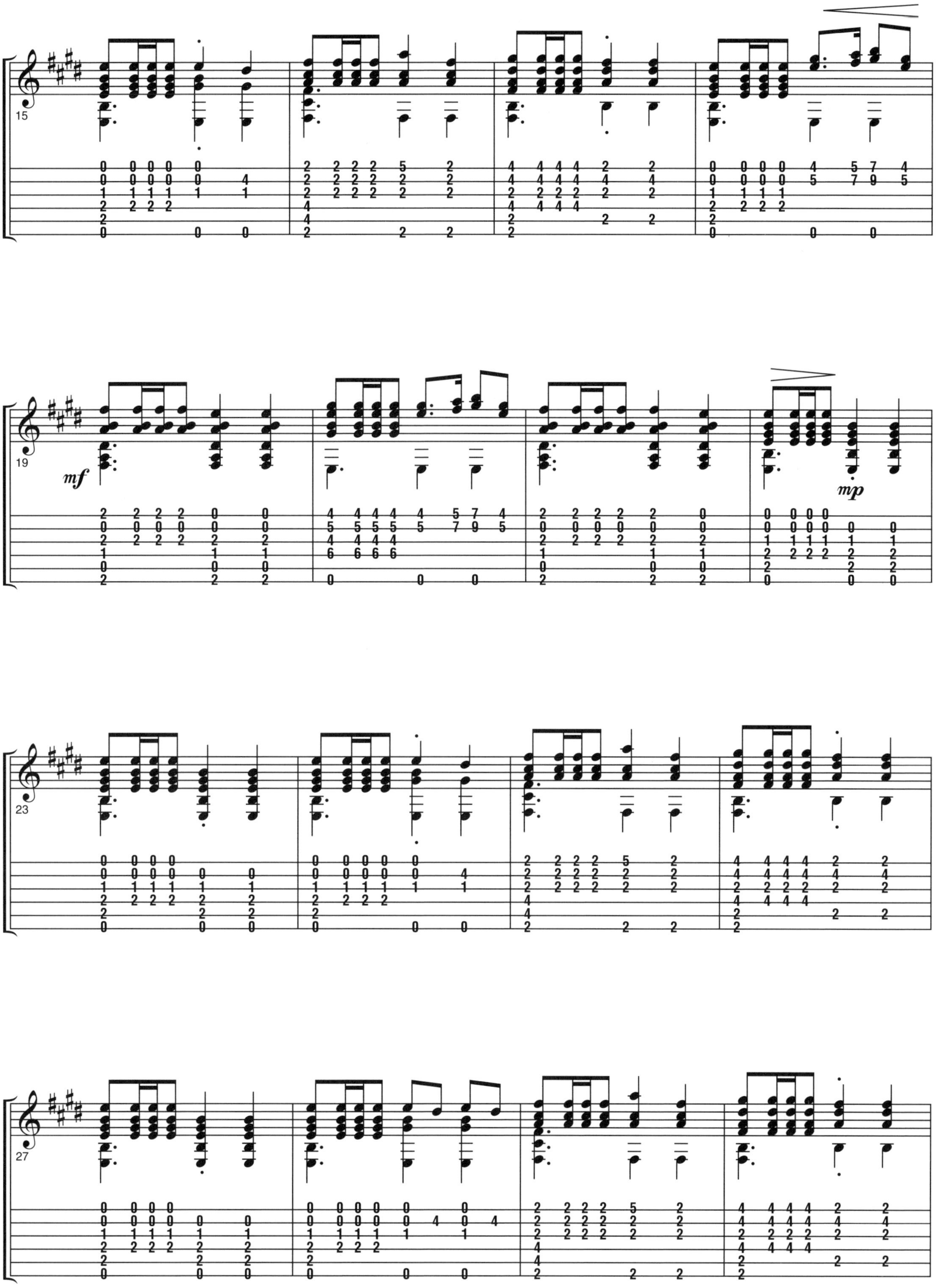
15
19
mf
mp
23
27

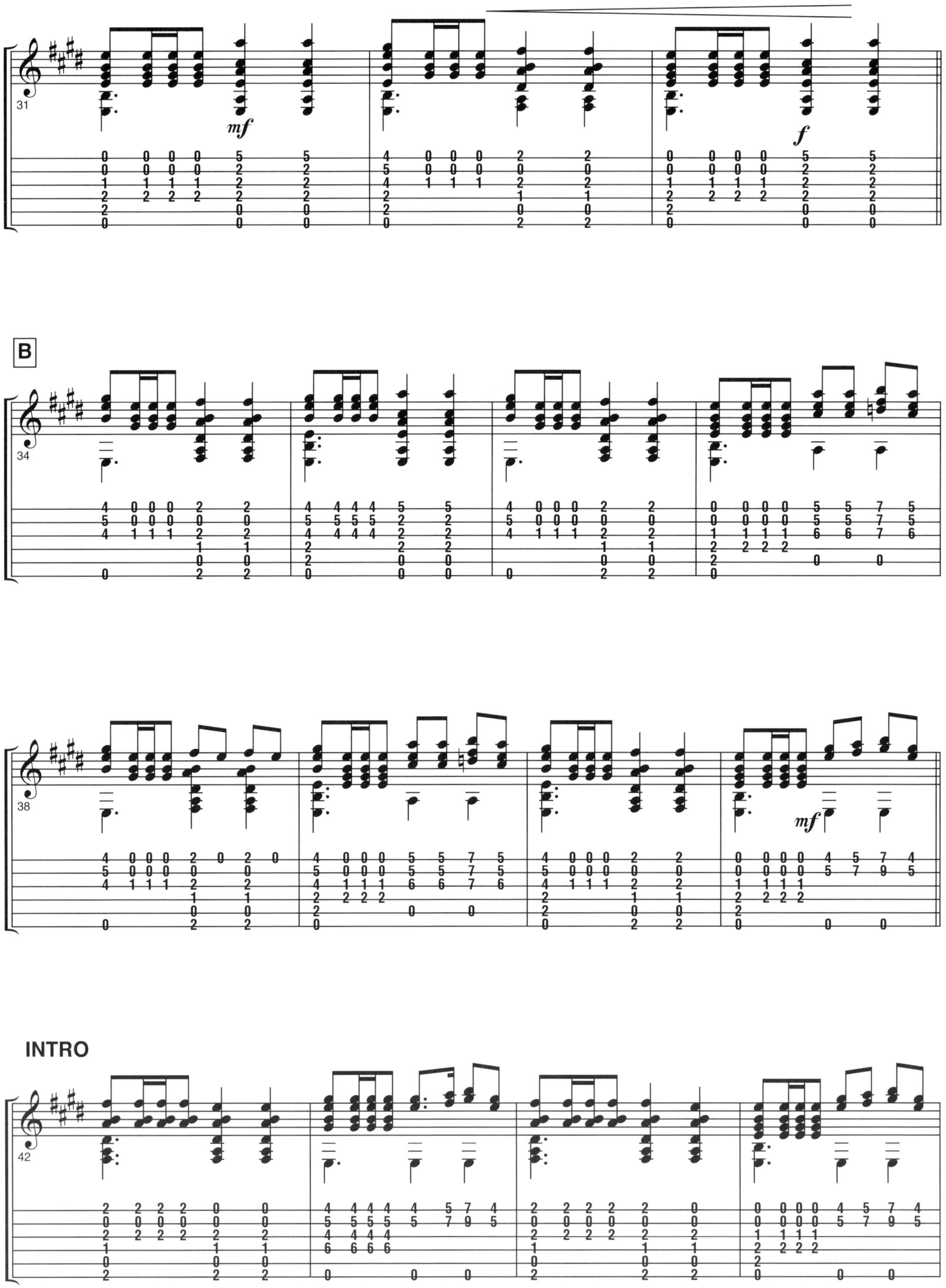
31
mf
f
B
34
38
mf
INTRO
42

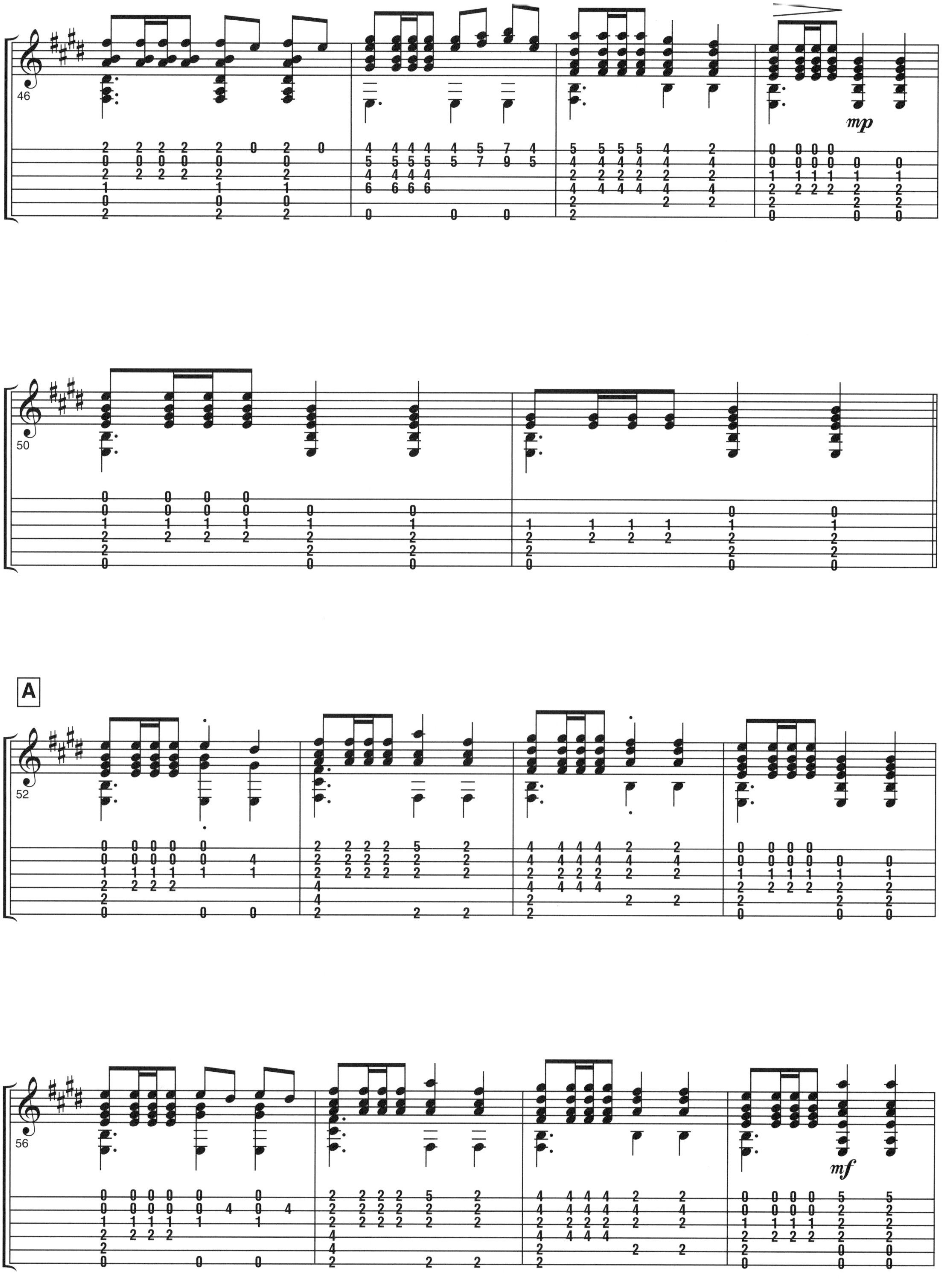
46
mp
50
A
52
56
mf

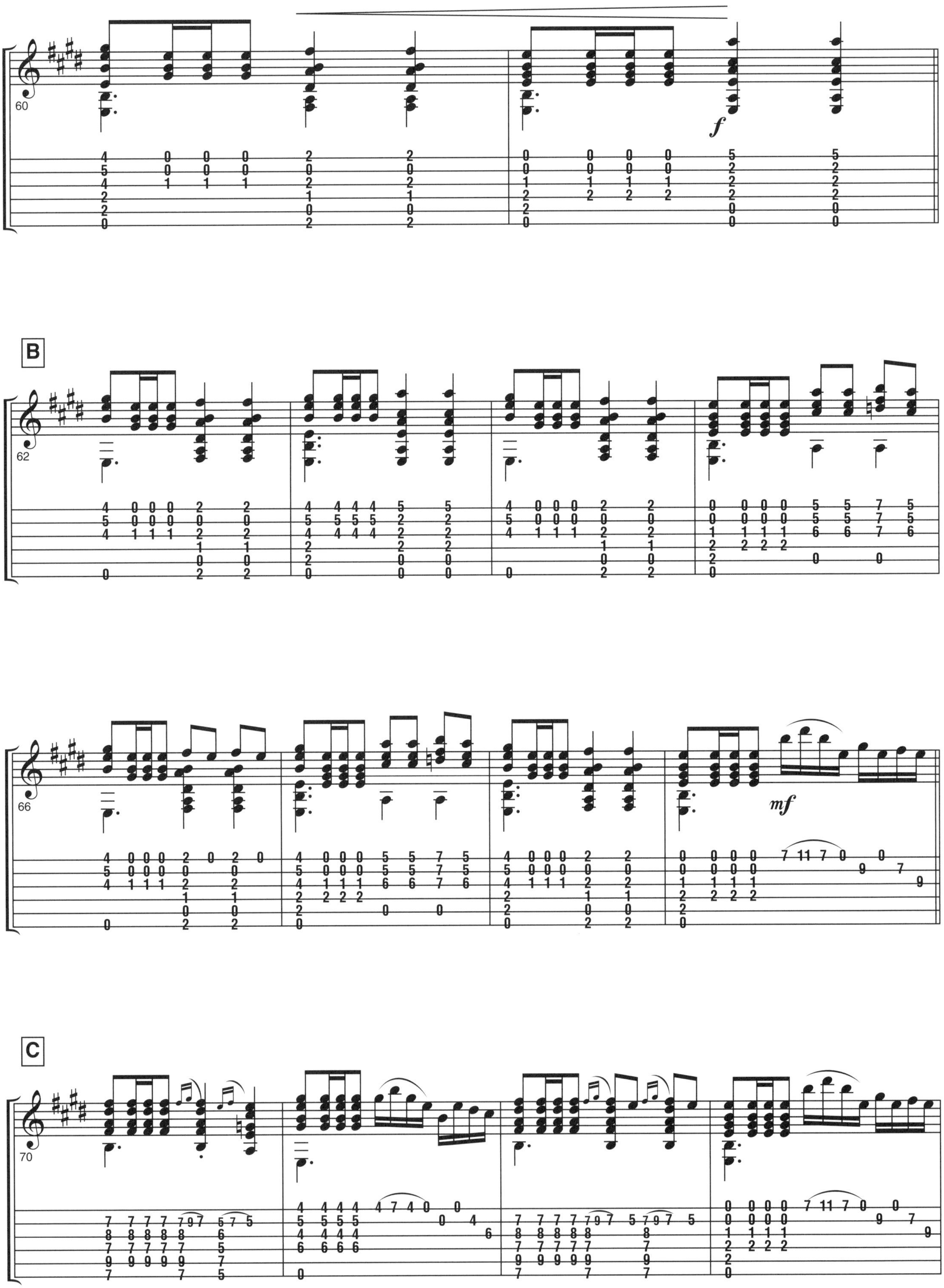
60
f
B
62
66
mf
C
70

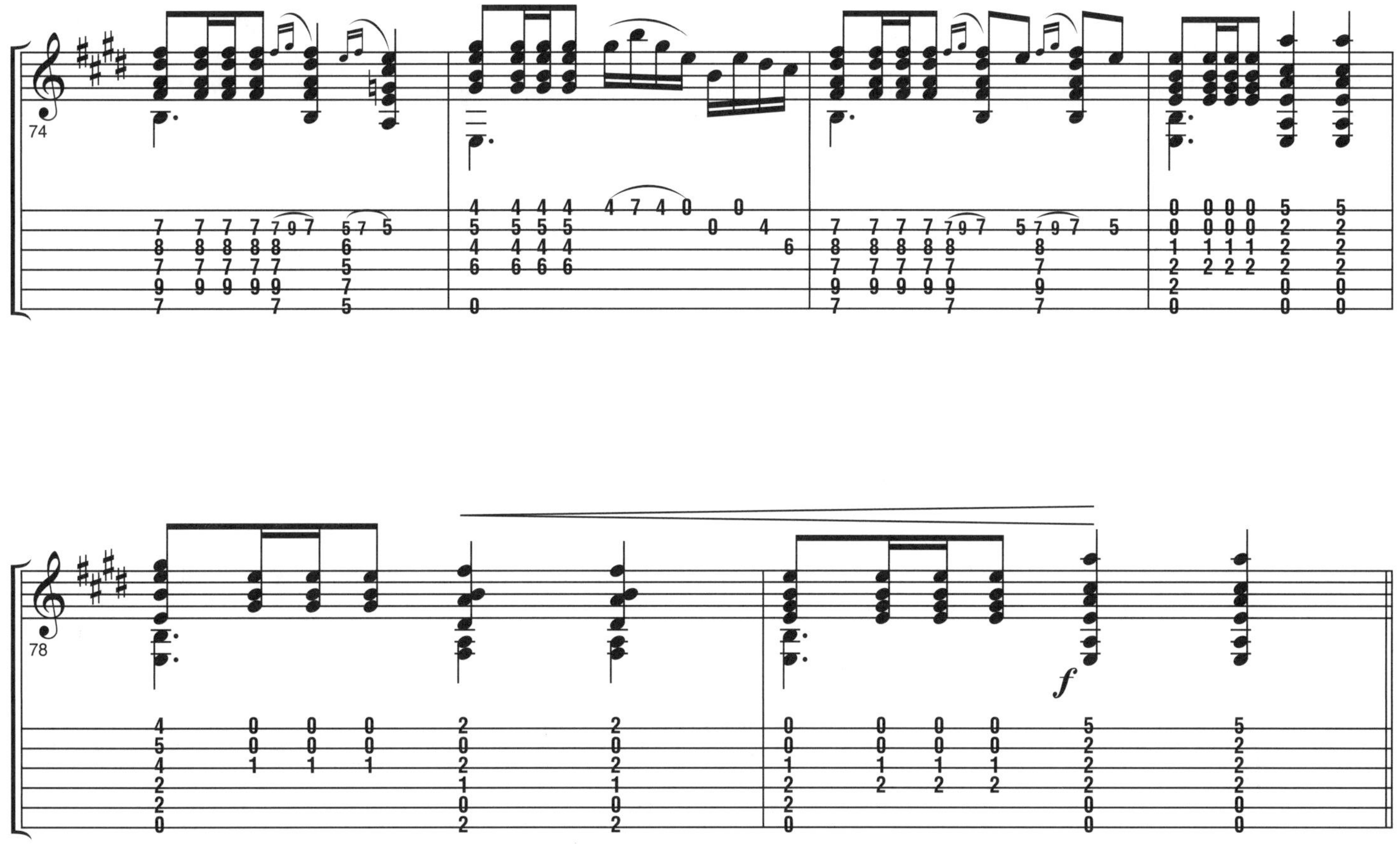

B **Double Time**

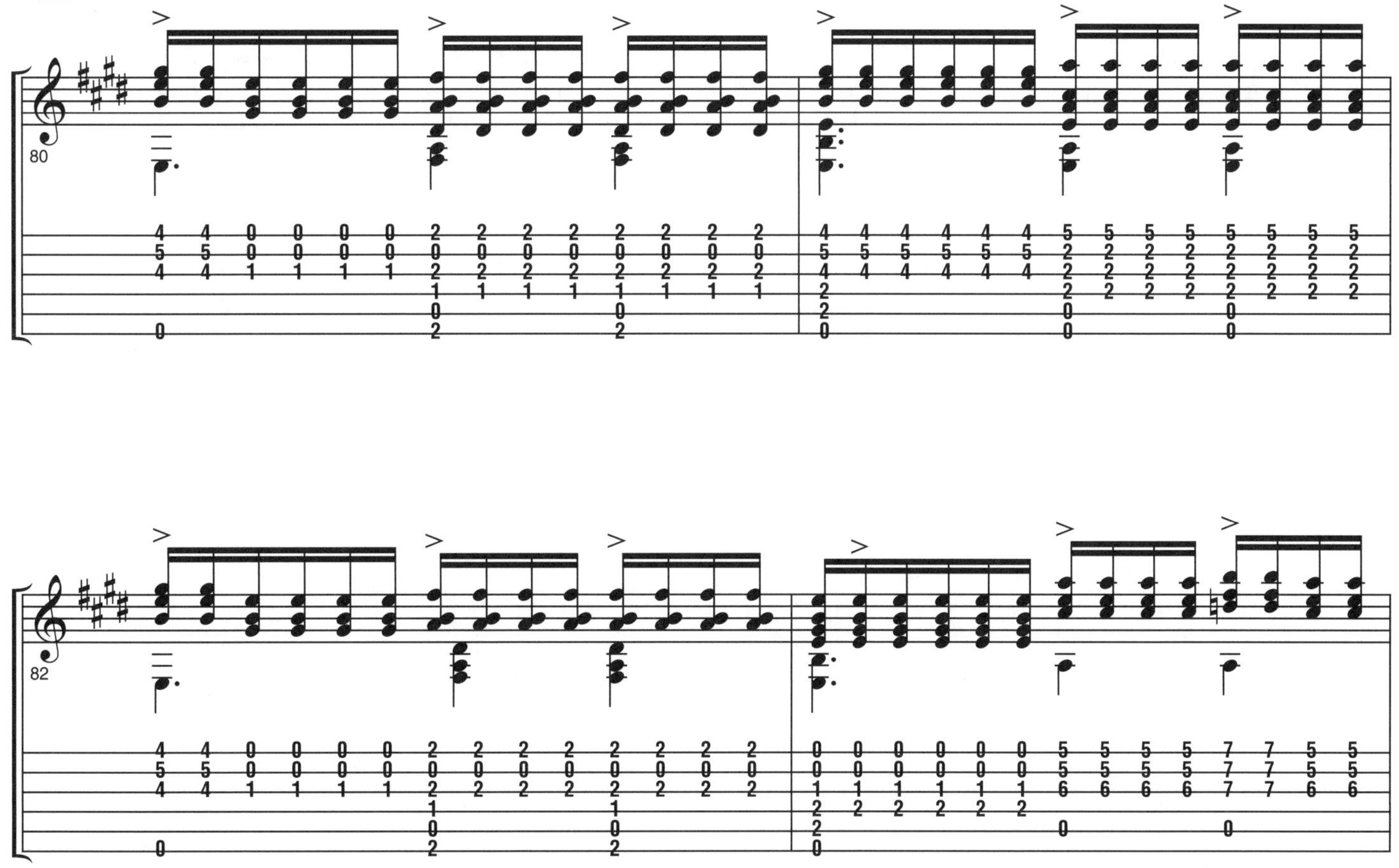

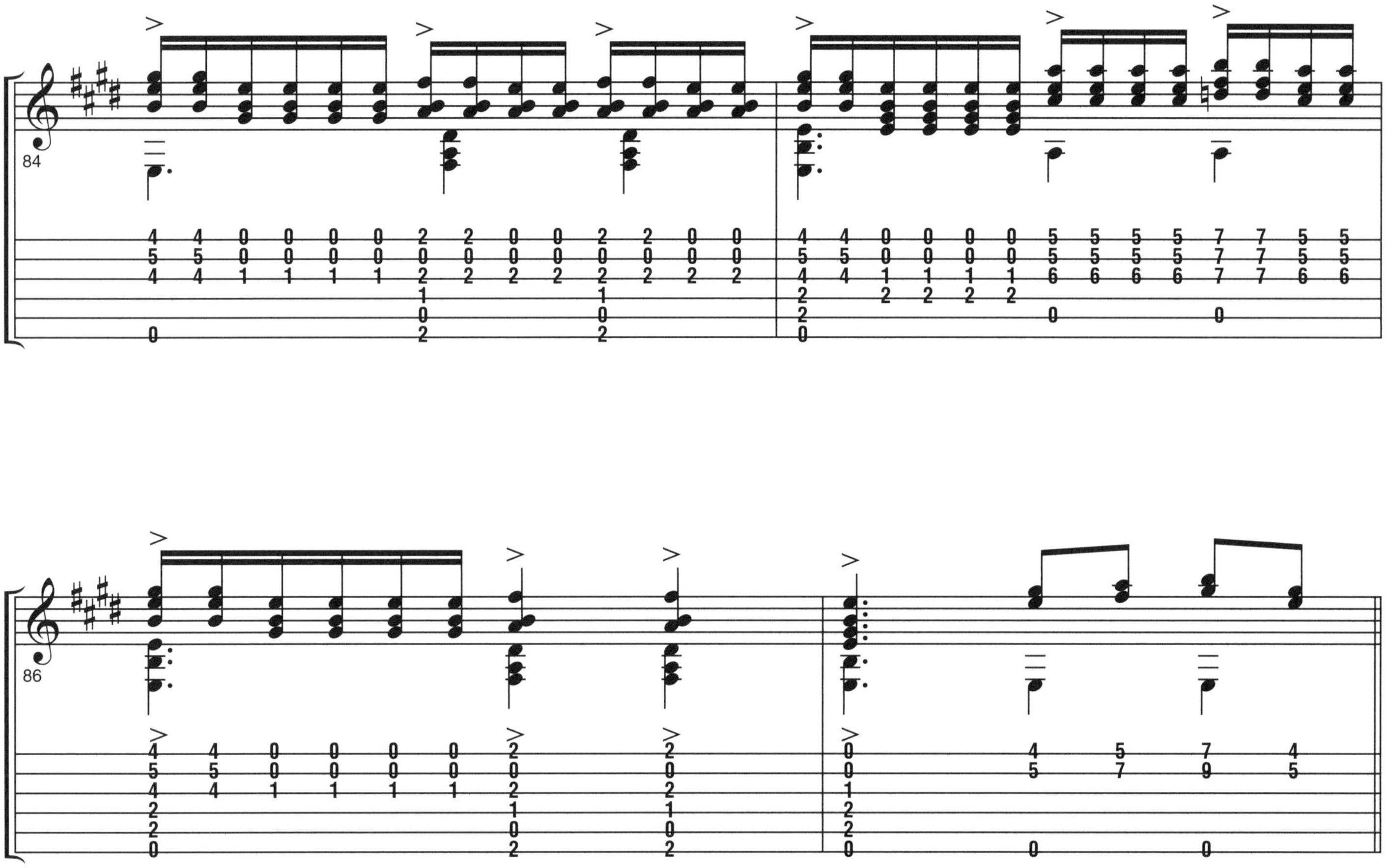

FINAL INTRO

TO BOUZOUKI MOU (MY BOUZOUKI)
(Zeybekiko)

Here is another Zeybekiko, but this time the same rhythm pattern starts from a different point. Do the same as before; practice only strumming the rhythm while you tap your foot. It should come easy since it is like the first Zeybekiko pattern, only shifted.

Example 25

To Bouzouki Mou

Zeybekiko

Composed by Fernando Pérez

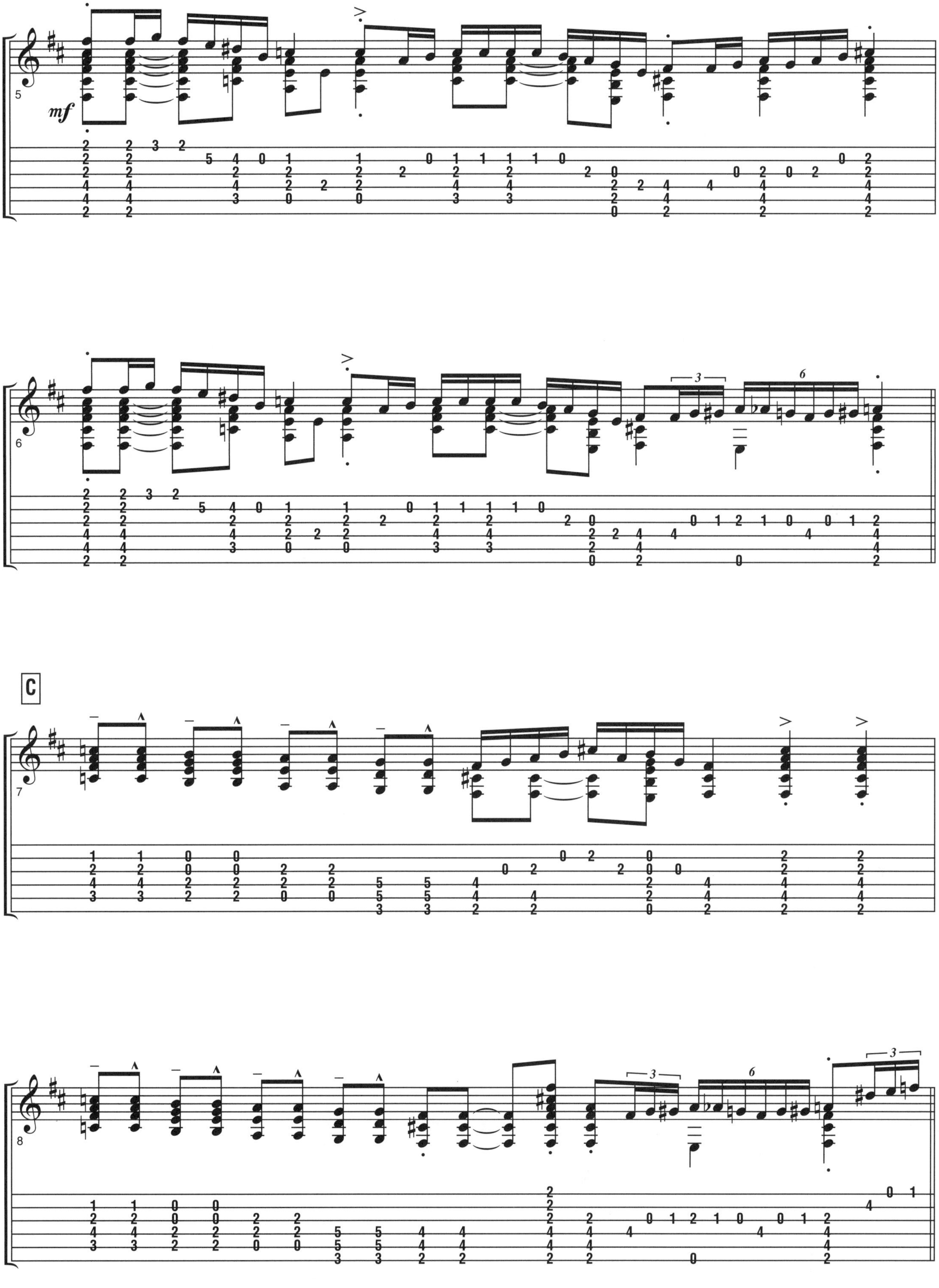
mf
C

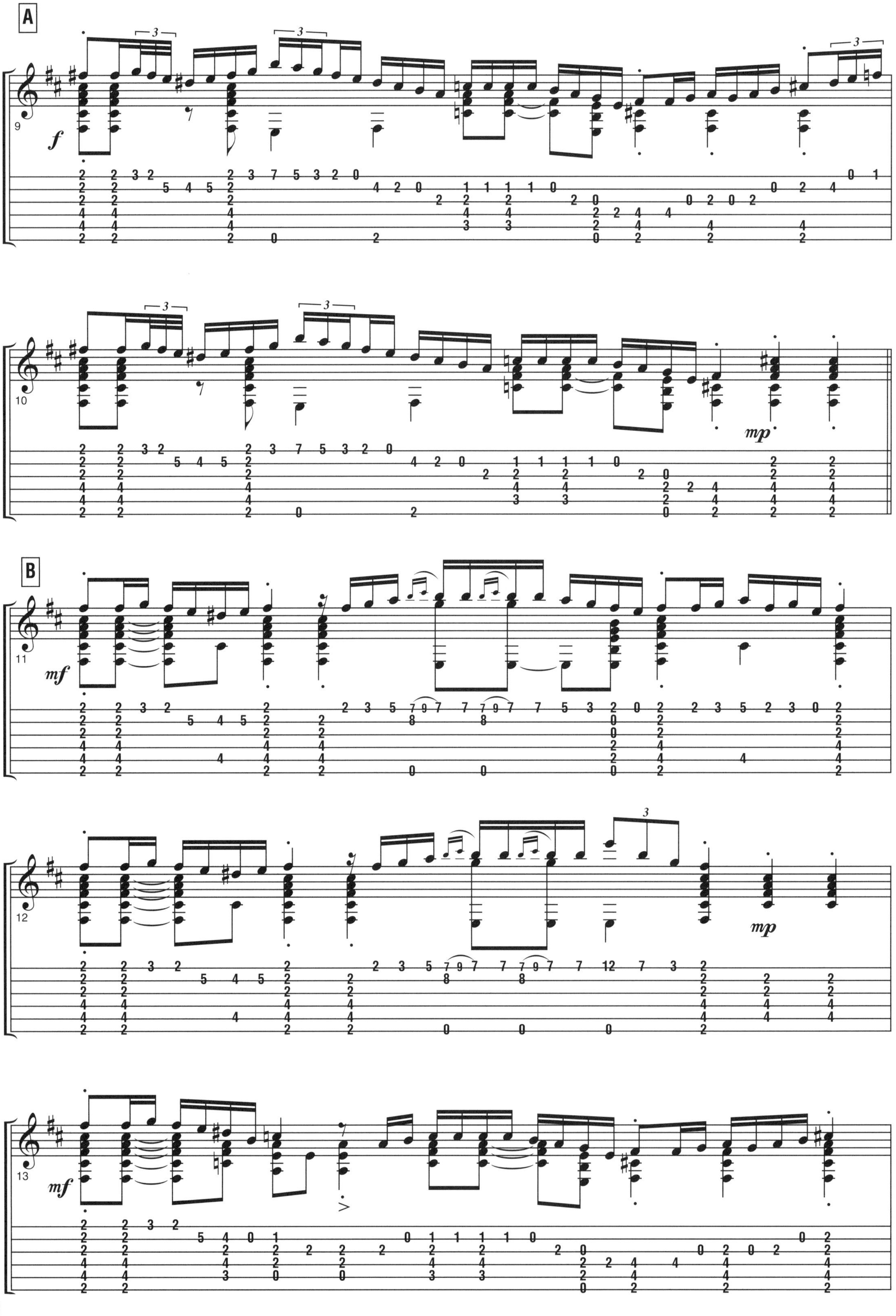
A
f
mp
B
mf
mp
mf

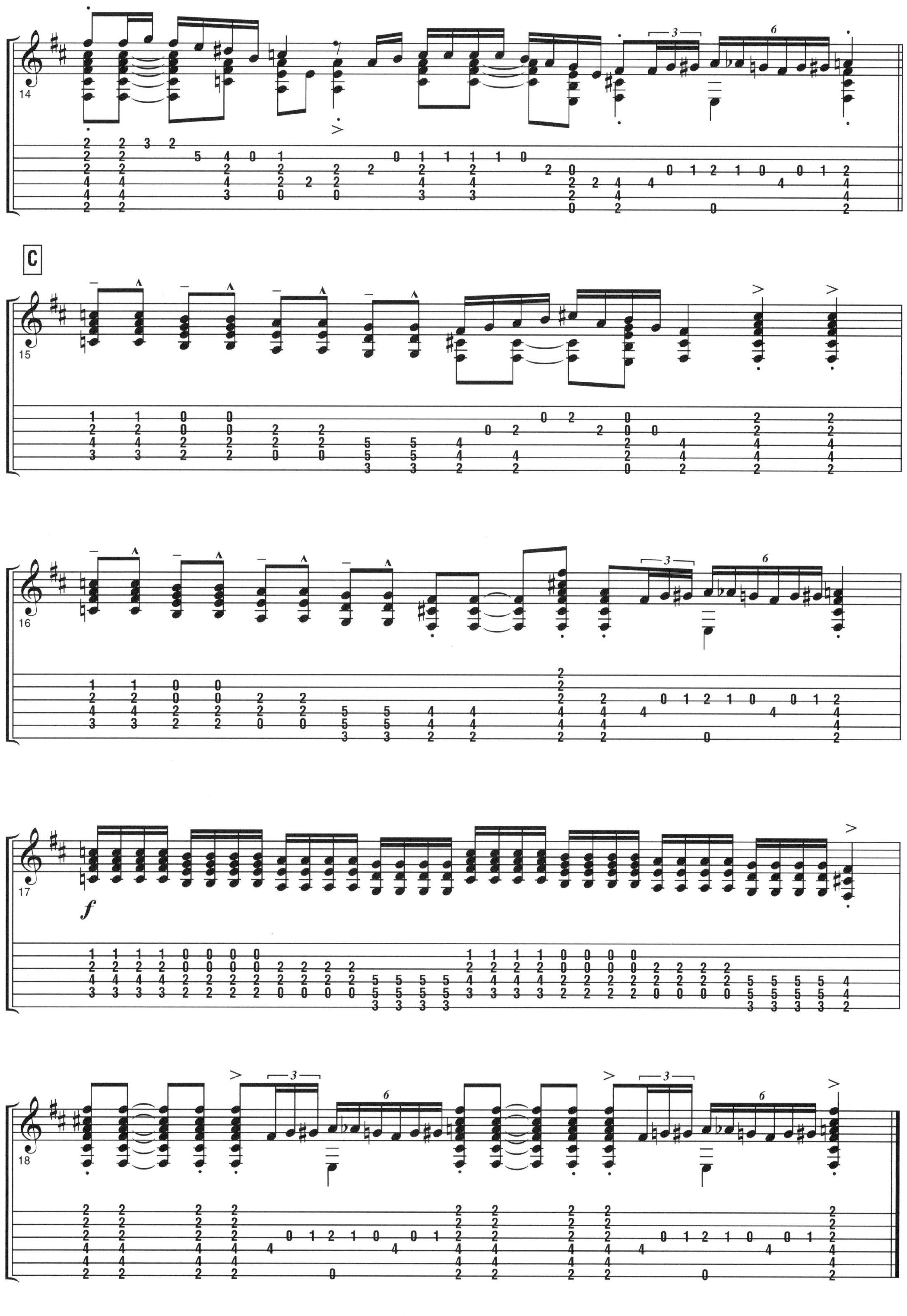
C
f

EPIRUS DANCE

This dance from Epirus is also known as Zagorisios. It looks a little tricky at the beginning, but after you study the melody, it will seem easier. It starts in a 5/4 time signature divided as 2+3. Practice it strumming only one chord with a rhythm like this:

Example 26

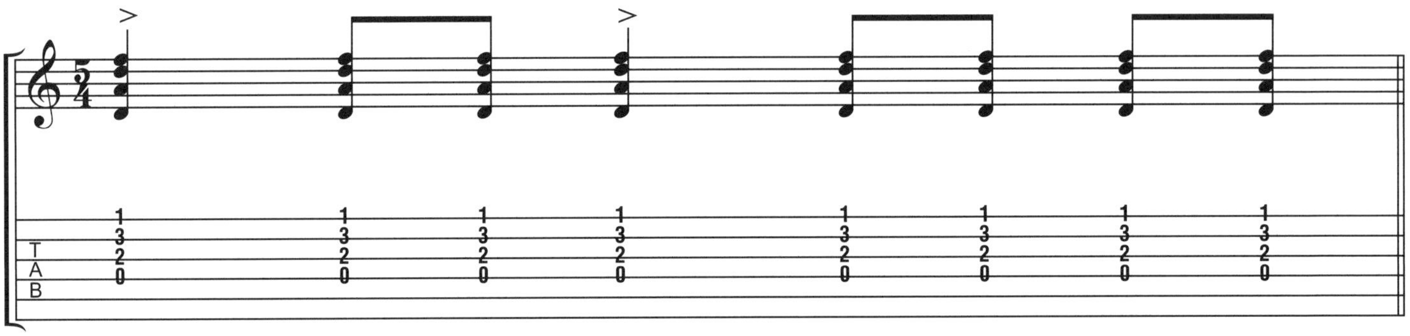

After the main melodies, it is typical to change to a Tsikisto rhythm towards the end. Practice it strumming one chord, but remember that Tsikisto will be played much faster.

Example 27

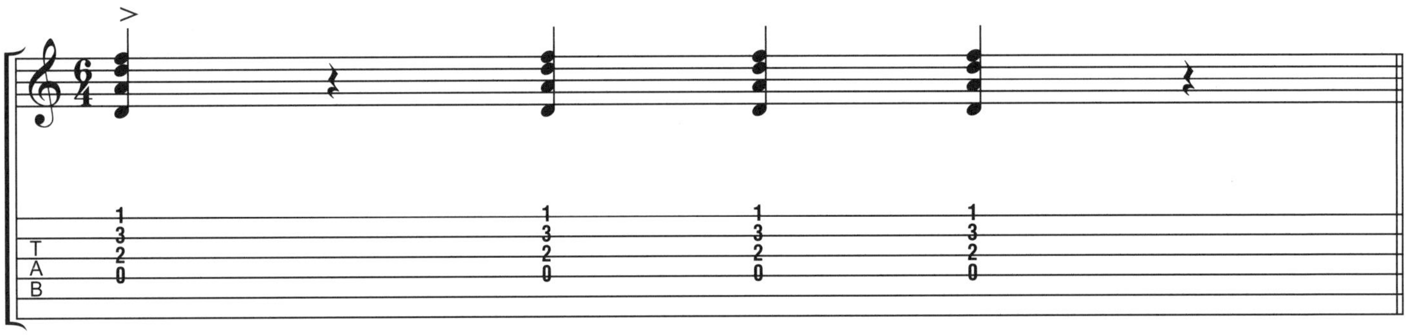

Don't forget to tune the sixth string down to D for this song.

Epirus Dance

(Zagorisios, Tsikisto)

Tune 6th string to D

Composed by Fernando Pérez

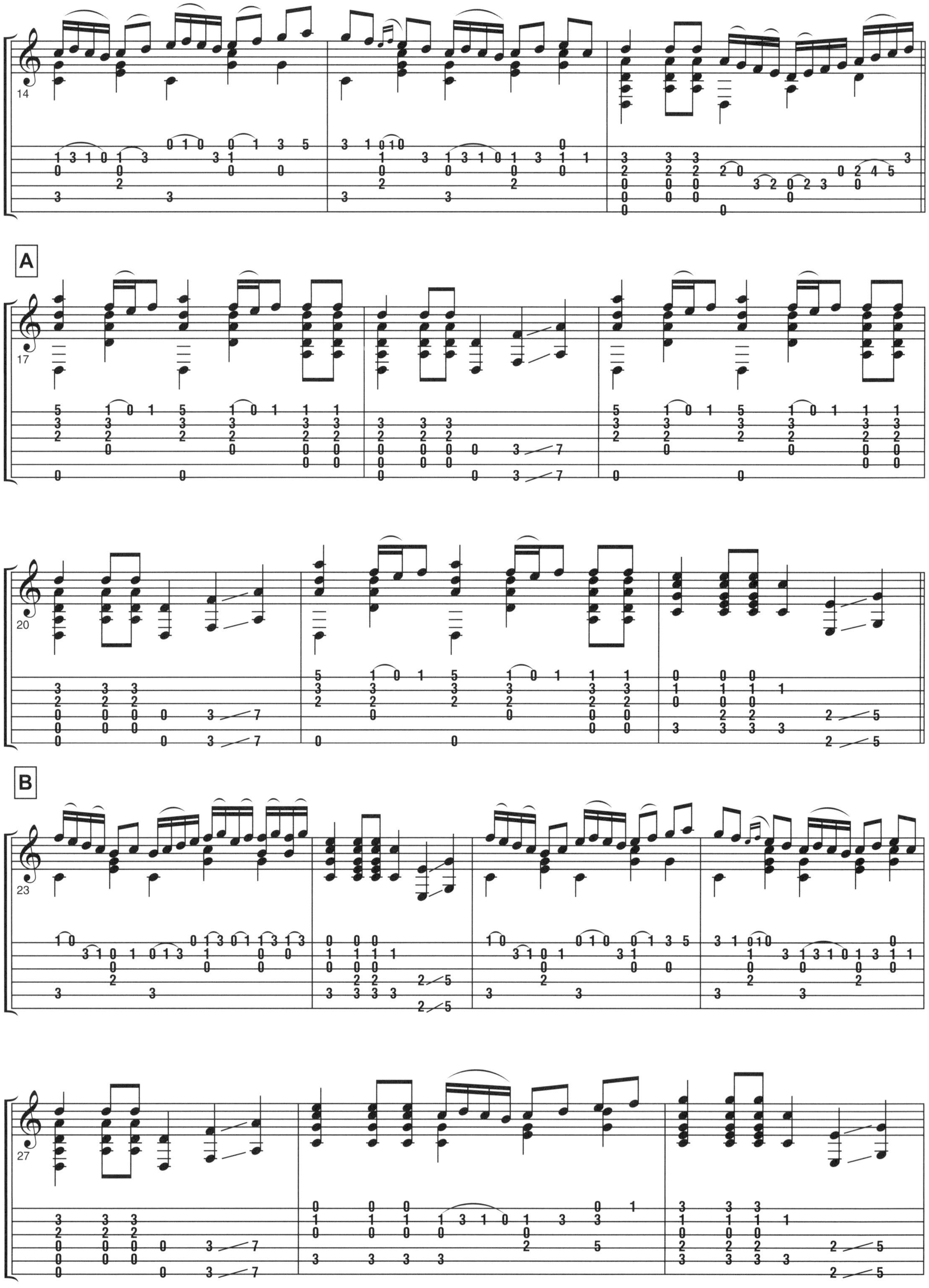
14
A
17
20
B
23
27

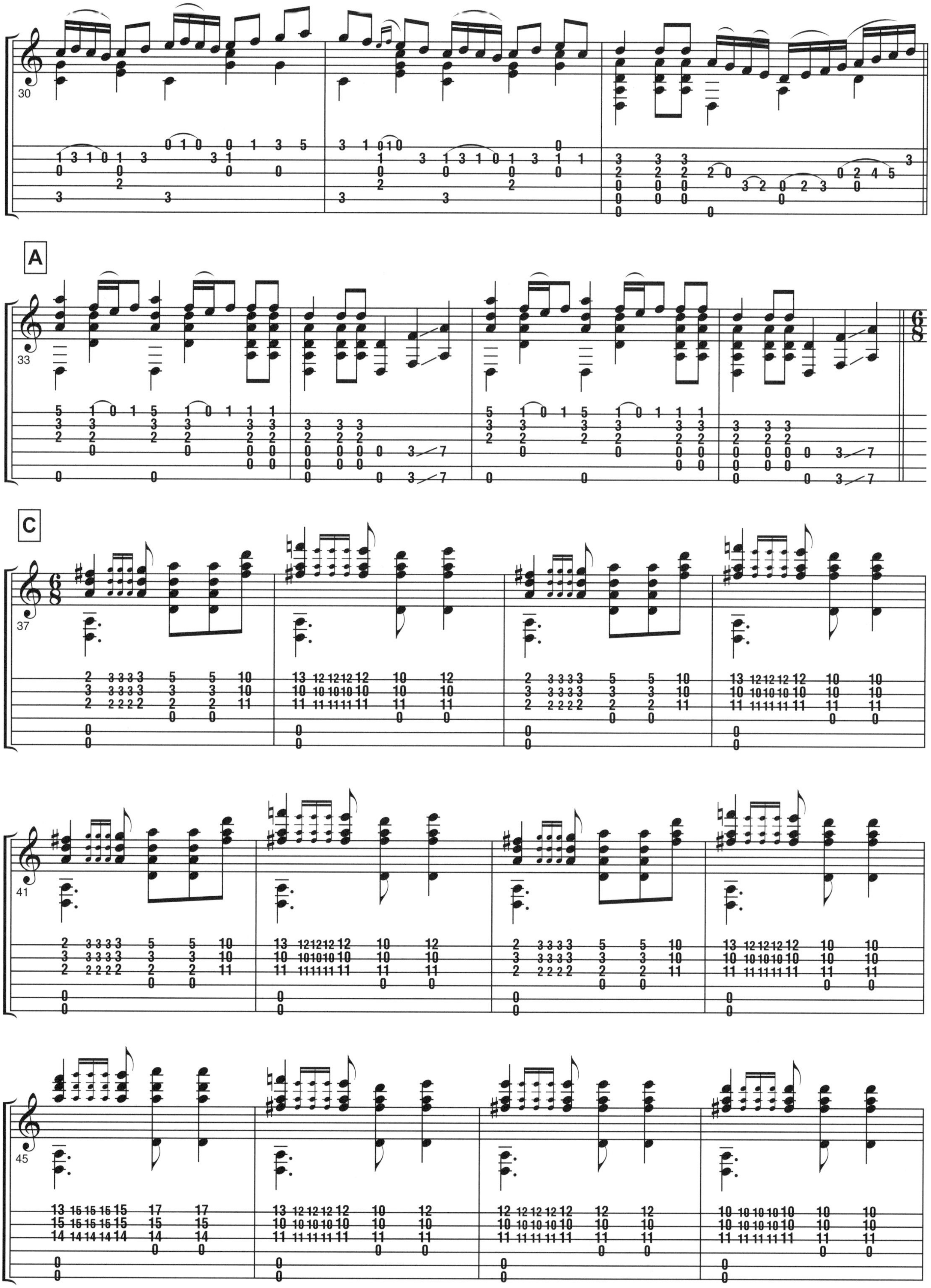
A
C

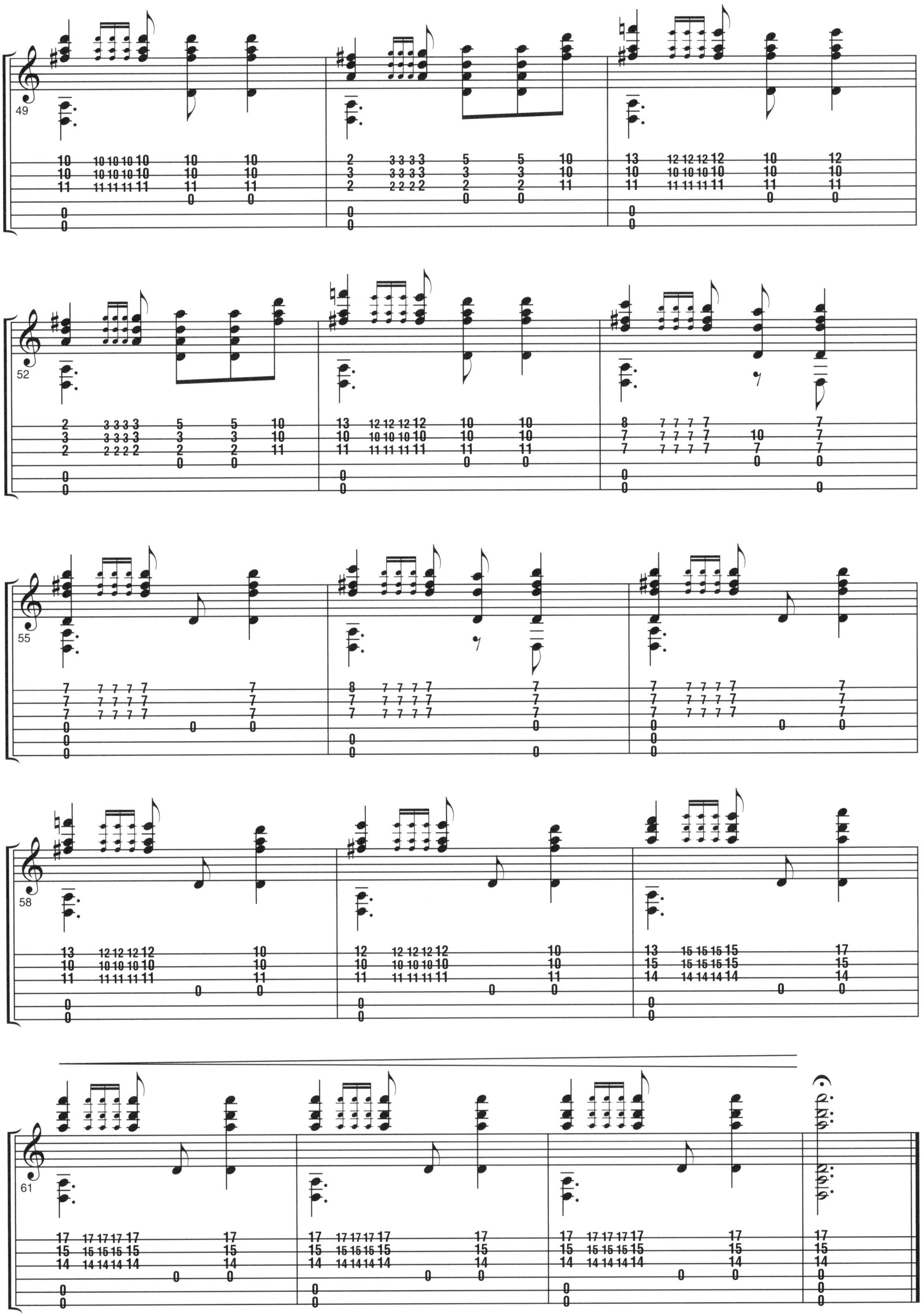
49
52
55
58
61

THESSALY DANCE
(Karagouna)

This is a guitar composition based on the airs of a well-known dance from Thessaly. It is also known as Karagouna, which refers to the farmers in the plains of Thessaly.

The score is written in 8/8, and the piece maintains a *dactyl* (Dactylos) rhythm, which is a long-short-short pattern. The best way to feel it would be to count "1234, 12,12". The foot taps only the 1 of every count. Try to not speed up the tempo; it's a heavy feel groove.

Example 28

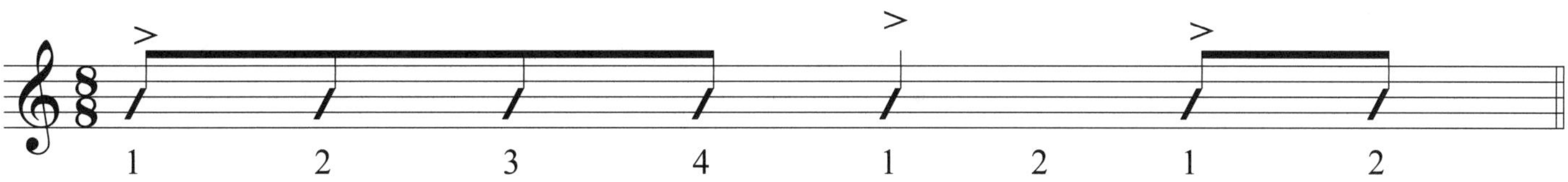

This tune is also in drop D tuning, so you need to tune the sixth string down to D.

Thessaly Dance

Karagouna

Tune 6th string to D

Composed by Fernando Pérez

17
p
B
19
mf
22
25
p

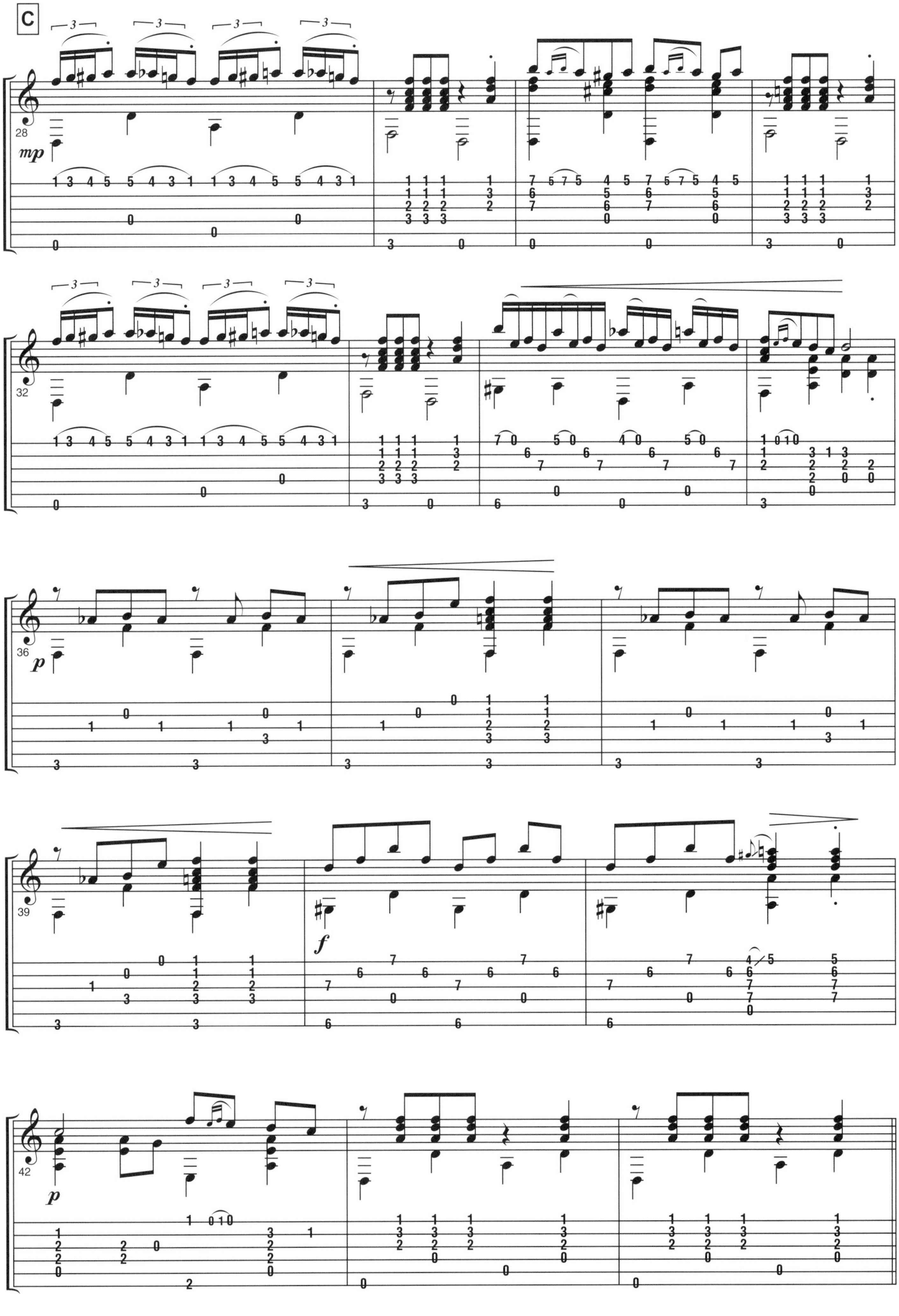
C
mp
p
f
p

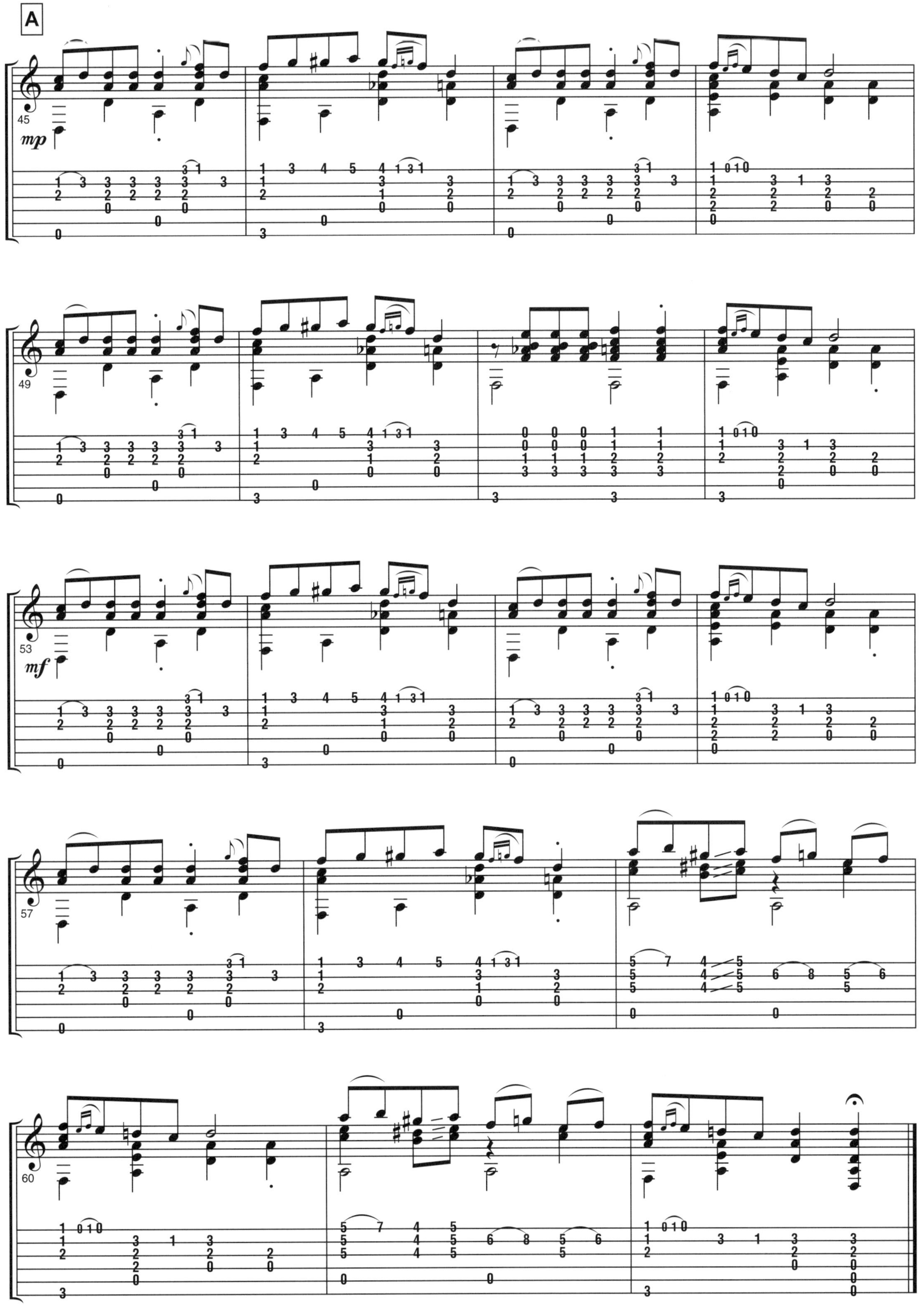
A
45
mp
49
53
mf
57
60

BALKAN KALAMATIANOS

Here is another Kalamatianos especially written for guitar. In fact, the tempo here is much faster than a usual Kalamatianos. Also, the melody has a northern feel, similar to ones in the Balkans area.

If you worked on the earlier Kalamatianos ("The Shoemaker's Shoe"), you can go ahead and try this one. Otherwise, I recommend that you check the preparation exercise written there to get used to a 7/8 meter. This piece is also capoed at fret 3.

Balkan Kalamatianos

Composed by Fernando Pérez

Capo III

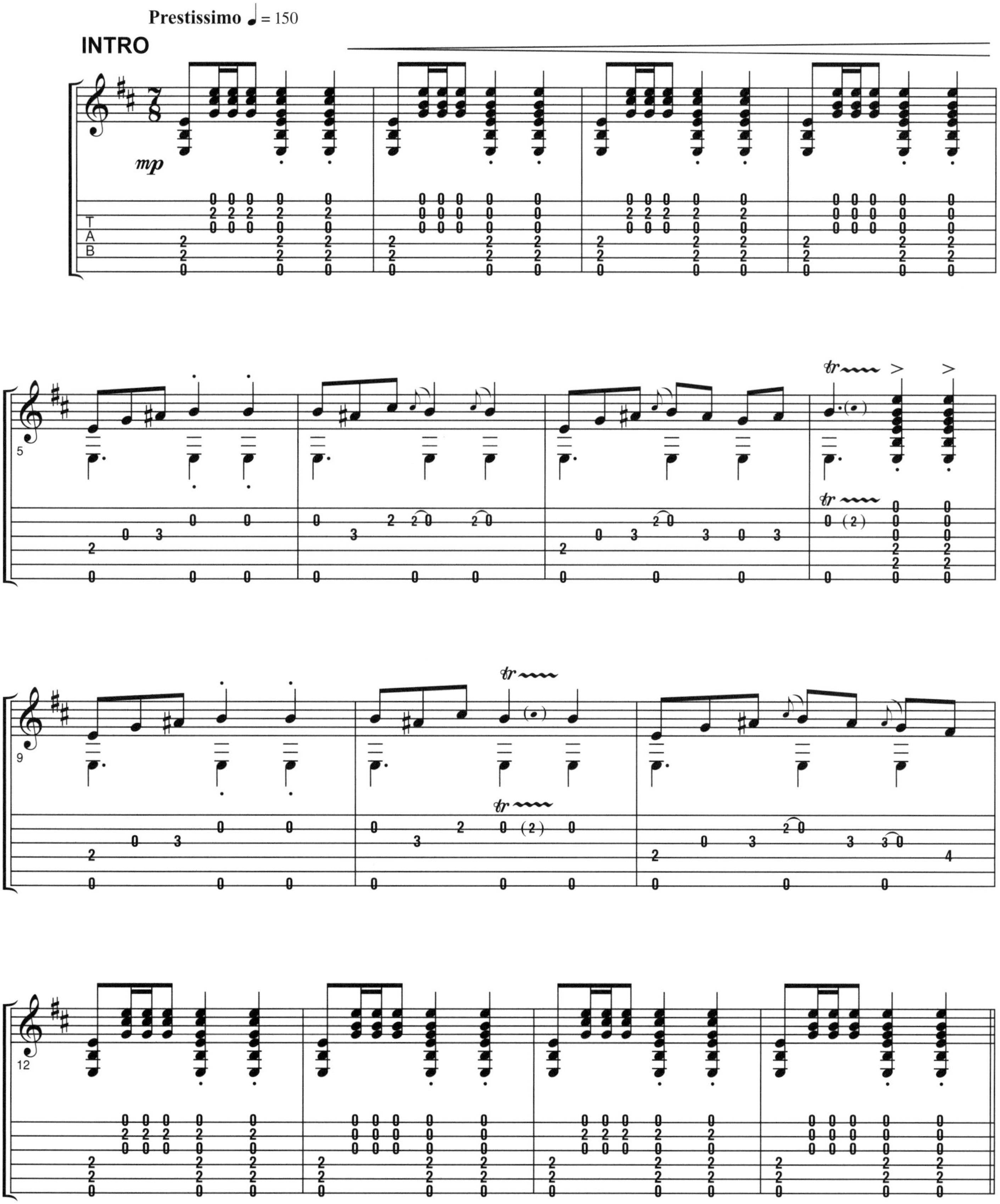

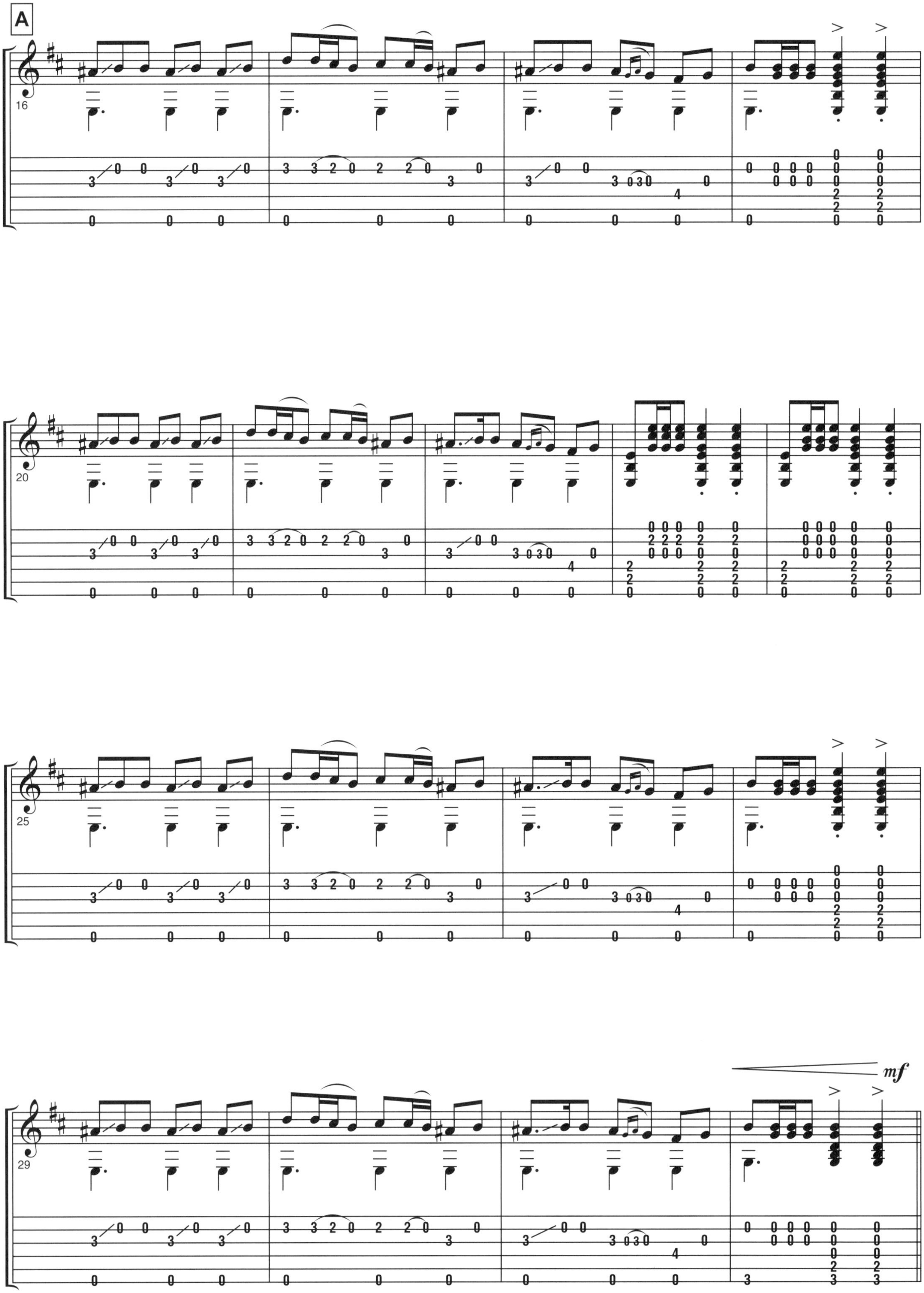
A
16
20
25
29
mf

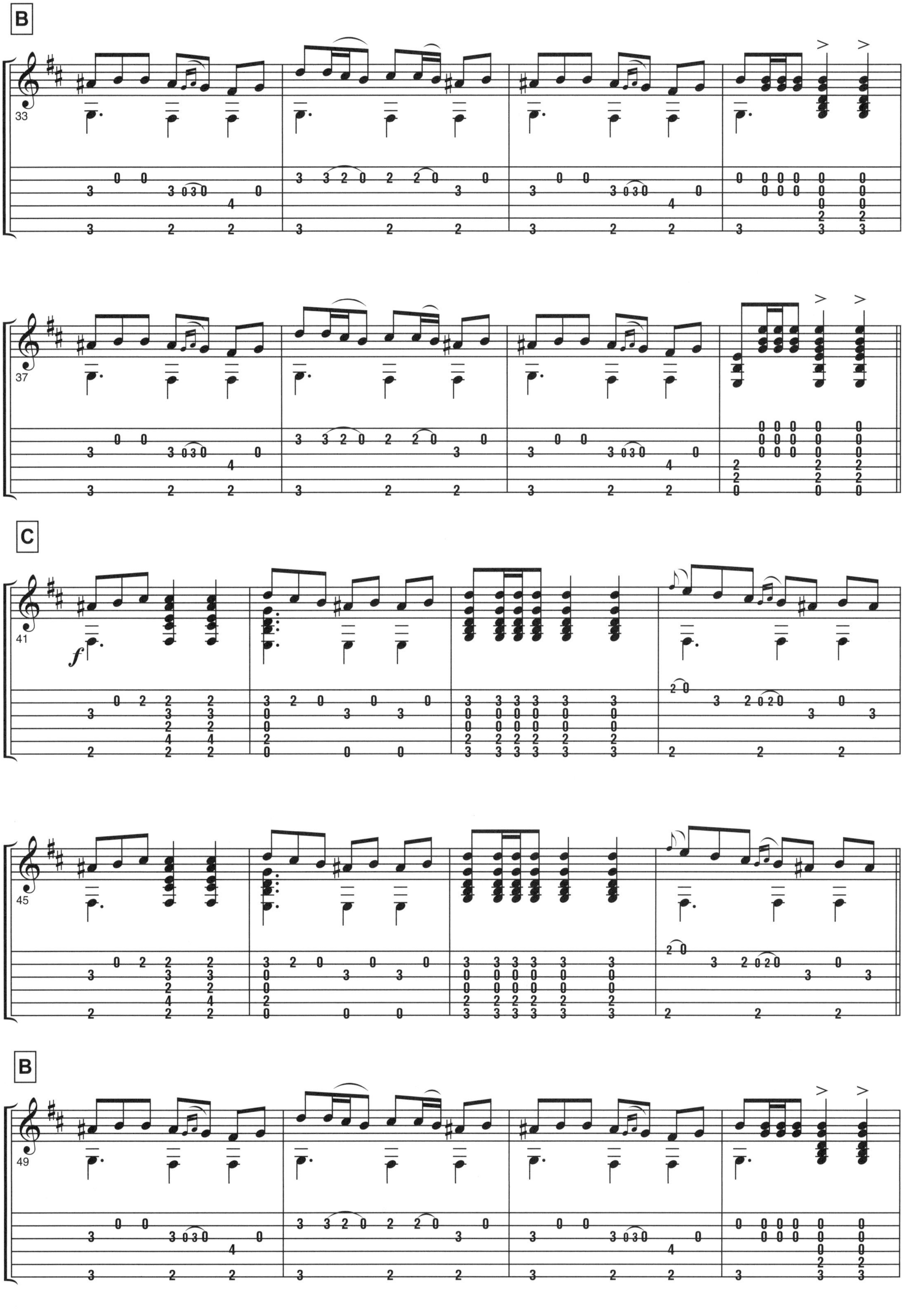
B
33
37
C
41
45
B
49

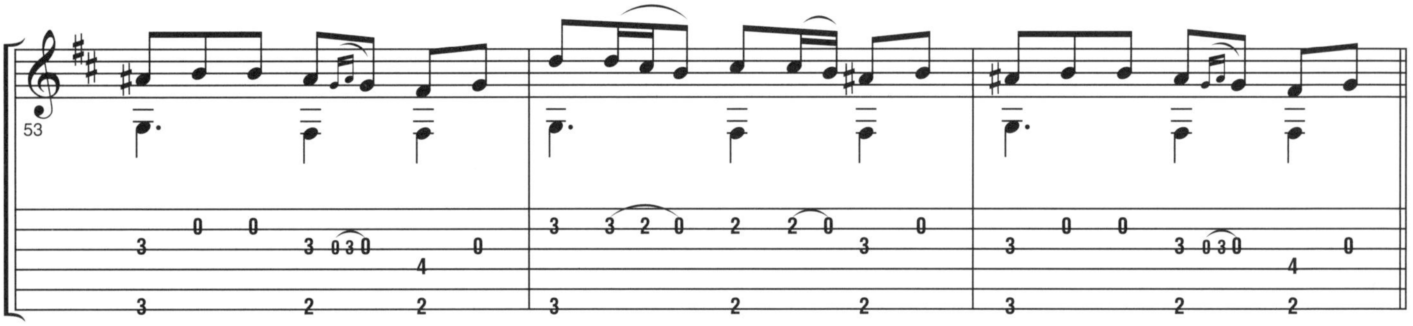

FINAL INTRO

KASTRO PSILO O EROTAS
(HIGH CASTLE OF LOVE)
(Cretan Mantinada)

This tune has a melody based on Cretan airs. The composition comes originally from writing music to a Mantinada, which is a poetic form with origins in the Venetian Matinada that became popular in Crete at the end of the 14th century.

The rhythm is sort of a Tsifteteli, which is a common rhythm found in the Greek belly dance, but in a slower version. Only the intro has a variation in the rhythm; the verses return to a normal Tsifteteli.

Here is a simple example of the Tsifteteli rhythmic pattern:

Example 29

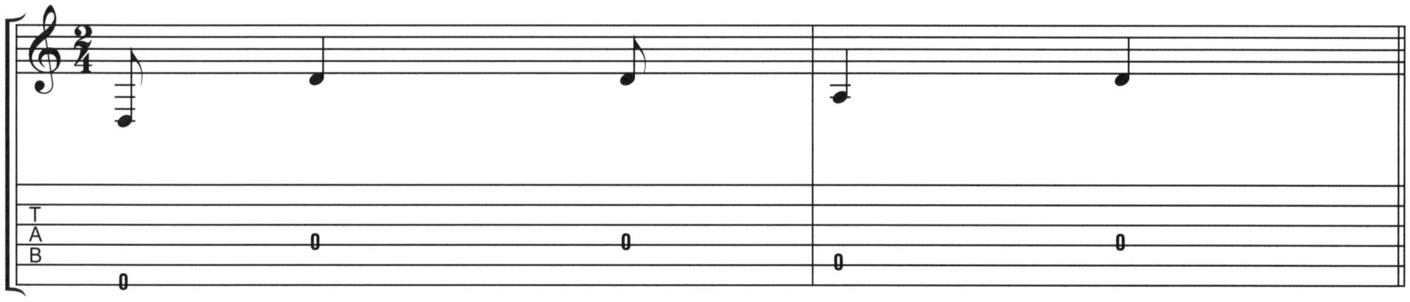

Originally, this melody was played on a fretless guitar imitating the oud sound.

This is also more convenient because, in the melody, sometimes the E♭ is tuned slightly lower. On the standard guitar, I have chosen to play the normal E♭. On the other hand, I am keeping the oud tuning so that it becomes more natural to play the ornaments. The tuning is, from sixth to first string: DADGCF. But don't panic; in reality, this is a small change. The sixth string goes down to D as in drop D tuning. The only change in the rest of the strings happens on the second and first, both of which go up a half step.

Kastro Psilo o Erotas

Cretan Mantinada

Guitar Tuning: DADGCF

Composed by Fernando Pérez

INTRO

Andante ♩ = 85

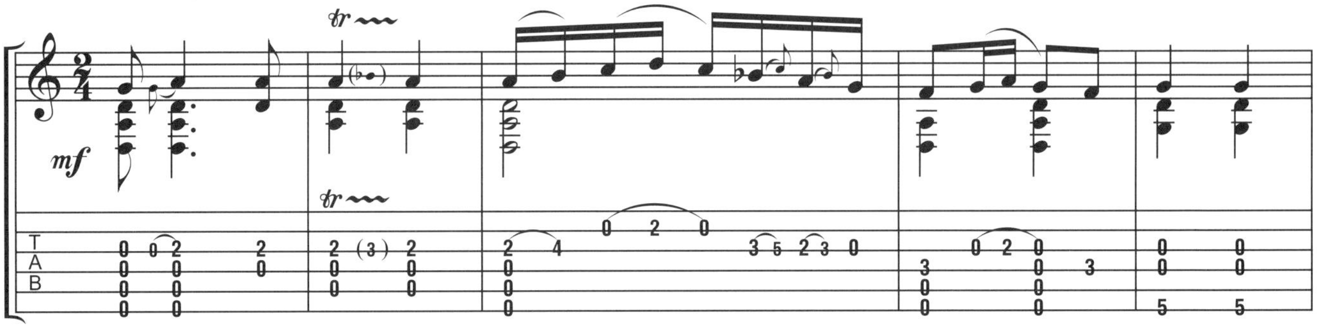

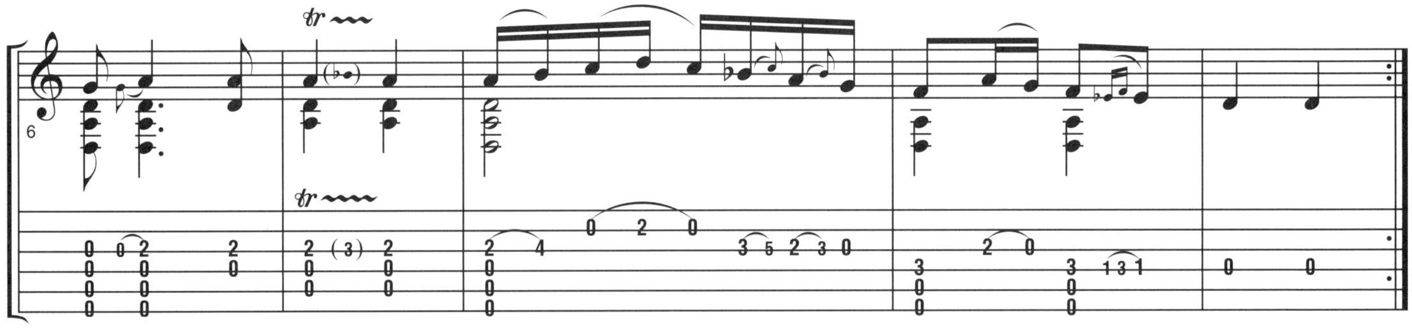

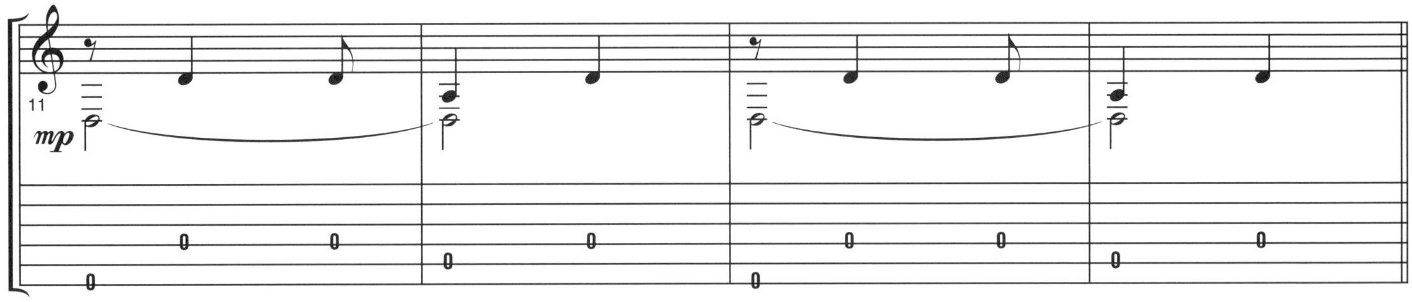

A

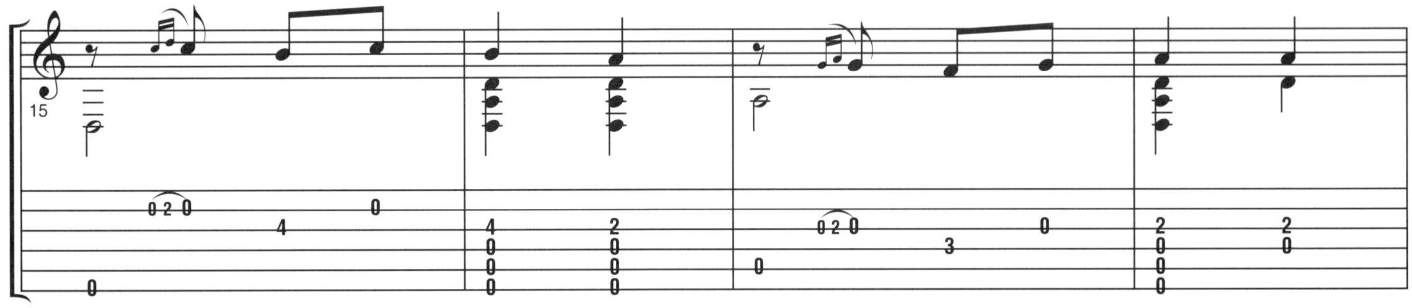

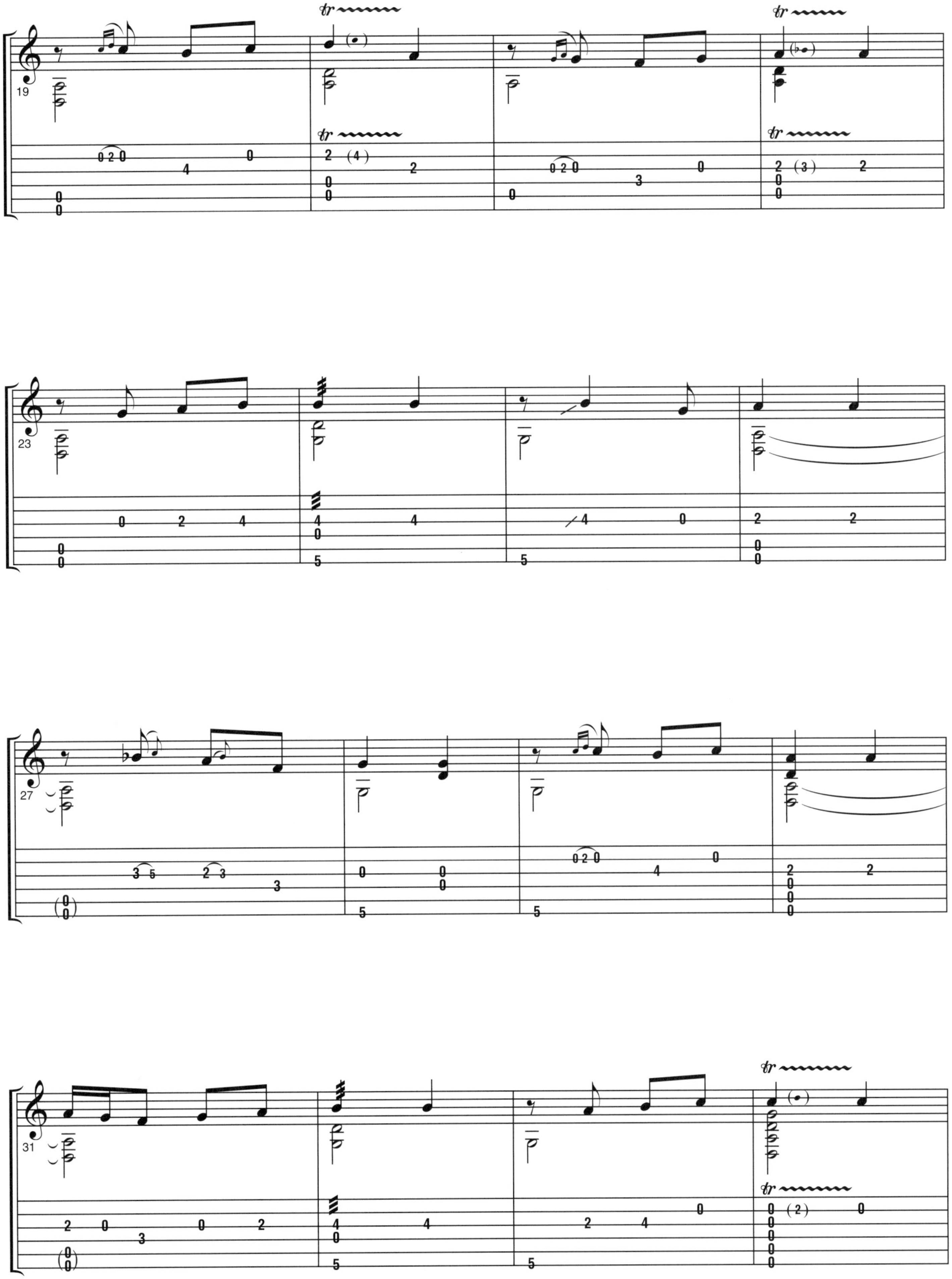
19
23
27
31

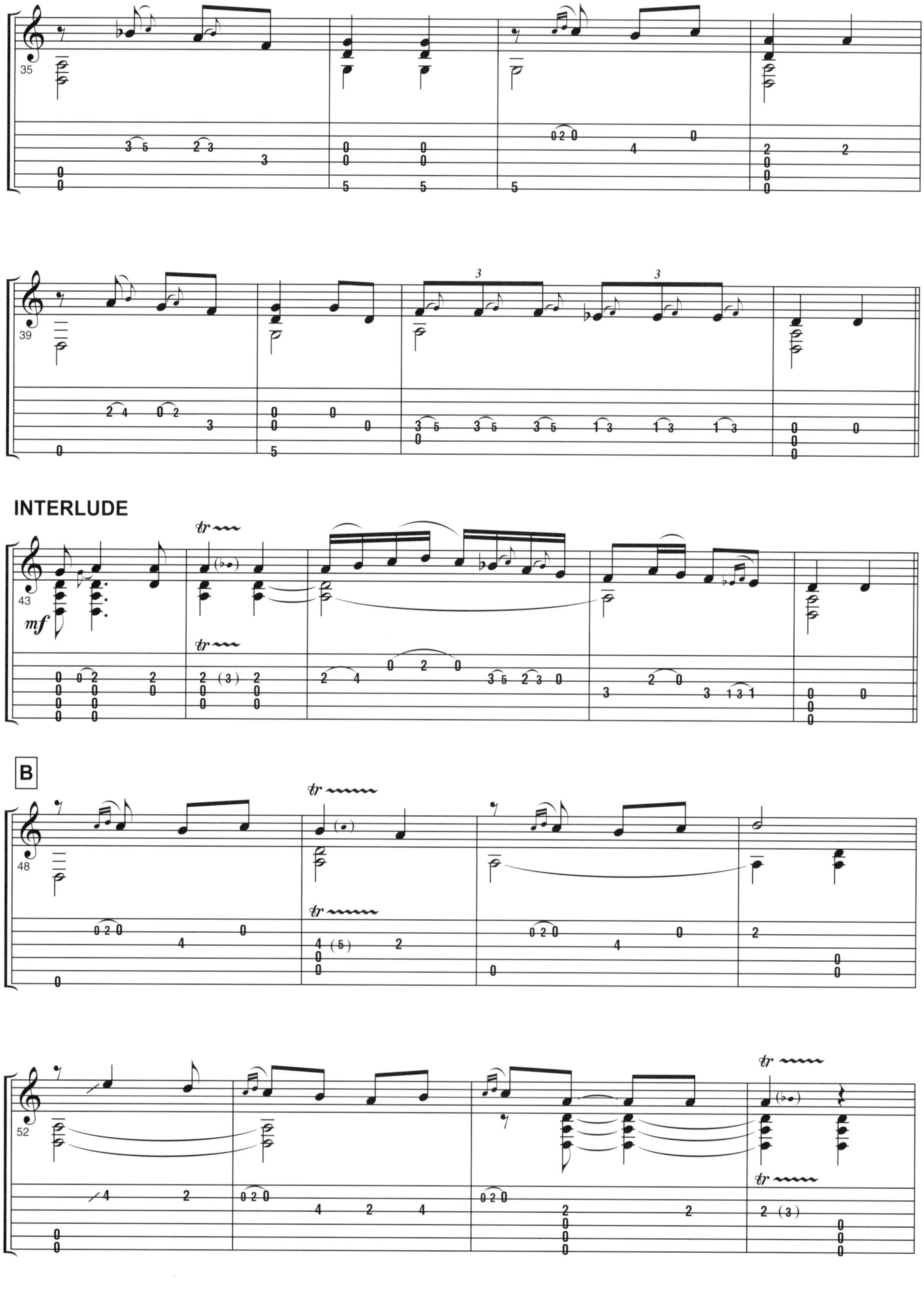
35
39
INTERLUDE
43
mf
tr
B
48
52

FINAL INTRO

ABOUT THE AUTHOR

Born in the town of Ejea de los Caballeros, Zaragoza, Fernando Perez's musical studies began at the age of seven. His first contact with classical music was in the conservatory of Spain. Following were numerous private instructors and music centers, including L'Aula de Musica in Barcelona, Escuela de Musica Creativa in Madrid, Musicians Institute in Hollywood, California, Maharaja Sawai Mansingh Sangeet Mahavidyalaya in Jaipur, India, Arabic Conservatoire de Musique d'Alexandrie in Egypt, Shanghai Conservatory of Music in China, and Labyrinth Music Center in Greece.

In these centers, he studied traditional, classical, and modern-contemporary music styles. But he's also spent time learning directly from artists and their cultures, traveling around the world to experience the spirit of different musical styles. Perez's talent and experience has led him to perform with artists from such exotic places as Hawaii, Cuba, Jamaica, West Africa, Japan, the Americas (South, Central, and North), Spain, France, Greece, Ireland, India, China, Turkey, Egypt, and many others.

The guitar has always been his passion, and he explores it in many forms, including Spanish classical guitar, dobro/resophonic, or other interesting ones like African guitar, Hawaiian ki Ho'alu (slack key) and Kika Kila (steel guitar), slide style from Mississippi, Flamenco, the curious way of playing guitar in Hindustani music found in India, or even the fretless Turkish and Arabic guitar. He also explores new horizons reflected in his arrangements and compositions based on instruments from many cultures, such as the Japanese koto, Chinese pipa and guqin, or African ngoni and kora.

His numerous performances in prestigious venues all around the world have turned Fernando Perez into one of the leading guitar artists who specialize in music from different cultures. He has several published works available representing the music of the major cultures of our planet performed on guitar. Often, he imparts master classes and workshops in different guitar festivals and music centers around the world as well as collaborates in musical research dealing with the subjects he knows best: guitar, music, and culture.

CLASSICAL GUITAR

PUBLICATIONS FROM HAL LEONARD

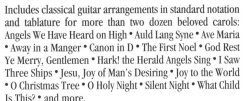

THE BEATLES FOR CLASSICAL GUITAR

Includes 20 solos from big Beatles hits arranged for classical guitar, complete with left-hand and right-hand fingering. Songs include: All My Loving • And I Love Her • Can't Buy Me Love • Fool on the Hill • From a Window • Hey Jude • If I Fell • Let It Be • Michelle • Norwegian Wood • Obla Di • Ticket to Ride • Yesterday • and more. Features arrangements and an introduction by Joe Washington, as well as his helpful hints on classical technique and detailed notes on how to play each song. The book also covers parts and specifications of the classical guitar, tuning, and Joe's "Strata System" – an easy-reading system applied to chord diagrams.

_______ 00699237 Classical Guitar $19.99

CZERNY FOR GUITAR

INCLUDES TAB

12 Scale Studies for Classical Guitar

by David Patterson

Adapted from Carl Czerny's *School of Velocity, Op. 299* for piano, this lesson book explores 12 keys with 12 different approaches or "treatments." You will explore a variety of articulations, ranges and technical perspectives as you learn each key. These arrangements will not only improve your ability to play scales fluently, but will also develop your ears, knowledge of the fingerboard, reading abilities, strength and endurance. In standard notation and tablature.

_______ 00701248 ....$10.95

MATTEO CARCASSI – 25 MELODIC AND PROGRESSIVE STUDIES, OP. 60

arr. Paul Henry

One of Carcassi's (1792-1853) most famous collections of classical guitar music – indispensable for the modern guitarist's musical and technical development. Performed by Paul Henry. 49-minute audio accompaniment.

_______ 00696506 Book/CD Pack $17.95

CLASSICAL & FINGERSTYLE GUITAR TECHNIQUES

INCLUDES TAB

by David Oakes • Musicians Institute

This Master Class with MI instructor David Oakes is aimed at any electric or acoustic guitarist who wants a quick, thorough grounding in the essentials of classical and fingerstyle technique. Topics covered include: arpeggios and scales, free stroke and rest stroke, P-i scale technique, three-to-a-string patterns, natural and artificial harmonics, tremolo and rasgueado, and more. The book includes 12 intensive lessons for right and left hand in standard notation & tab, and the CD features 92 solo acoustic tracks.

_______ 00695171 Book/CD Pack $17.99

CLASSICAL GUITAR CHRISTMAS COLLECTION

INCLUDES TAB

Includes classical guitar arrangements in standard notation and tablature for more than two dozen beloved carols: Angels We Have Heard on High • Auld Lang Syne • Ave Maria • Away in a Manger • Canon in D • The First Noel • God Rest Ye Merry, Gentlemen • Hark! the Herald Angels Sing • I Saw Three Ships • Jesu, Joy of Man's Desiring • Joy to the World • O Christmas Tree • O Holy Night • Silent Night • What Child Is This? • and more.

_______ 00699493 Guitar Solo $9.95

CLASSICAL GUITAR WEDDING

INCLUDES TAB

Perfect for players hired to perform for someone's big day, this songbook features 16 classsical wedding favorites arranged for solo guitar in standard notation and tablature. Includes: Air on the G String • Ave Maria • Bridal Chorus • Canon in D • Jesu, Joy of Man's Desiring • Minuet • Sheep May Safely Graze • Wedding March • and more.

_______ 00699563 Solo Guitar with Tab $10.95

CLASSICAL MASTERPIECES FOR GUITAR

INCLUDES TAB

27 works by Bach, Beethoven, Handel, Mendelssohn, Mozart and more transcribed with standard notation and tablature. Now anyone can enjoy classical material regardless of their guitar background. Also features stay-open binding.

_______ 00699312 ....$12.95

MASTERWORKS FOR GUITAR

INCLUDES TAB

Over 60 Favorites from Four Centuries
World's Great Classical Music

Dozens of classical masterpieces: Allemande • Bourree • Canon in D • Jesu, Joy of Man's Desiring • Lagrima • Malaguena • Mazurka • Piano Sonata No. 14 in C# Minor (Moonlight) Op. 27 No. 2 First Movement Theme • Ode to Joy • Prelude No. I (Well-Tempered Clavier).

_______ 00699503 ....$16.95

HAL•LEONARD® CORPORATION

7777 W. Bluemound Rd. P.O. Box 13819 Milwaukee, WI 53213

A MODERN APPROACH TO CLASSICAL GUITAR

by Charles Duncan

This multi-volume method was developed to allow students to study the art of classical guitar within a new, more contemporary framework. For private, class or self-instruction. Book One incorporates chord frames and symbols, as well as a recording to assist in tuning and to provide accompaniments for at-home practice. Book One also introduces beginning fingerboard technique and music theory. Book Two and Three build upon the techniques learned in Book One.

_______ 00695114 Book 1 – Book Only...............$6.99
_______ 00695113 Book 1 – Book/CD Pack $10.99
_______ 00695116 Book 2 – Book Only...............$6.99
_______ 00695115 Book 2 – Book/CD Pack $10.99
_______ 00699202 Book 3 – Book Only...............$7.95
_______ 00695117 Book 3 – Book/CD Pack $10.95
_______ 00695119 Composite Book/CD Pack.....$29.99

ANDRES SEGOVIA – 20 STUDIES FOR GUITAR

Sor/Segovia

20 studies for the classical guitar written by Beethoven's contemporary, Fernando Sor, revised, edited and fingered by the great classical guitarist Andres Segovia. These essential repertoire pieces continue to be used by teachers and students to build solid classical technique. Features a 50-minute demonstration CD.

_______ 00695012 Book/CD Pack $19.99
_______ 00006363 Book Only $7.99

THE FRANCISCO COLLECTION TÁRREGA

INCLUDES TAB

edited and performed by Paul Henry

Considered the father of modern classical guitar, Francisco Tárrega revolutionized guitar technique and composed a wealth of music that will be a cornerstone of classical guitar repertoire for centuries to come. This unique book/CD pack features 14 of his most outstanding pieces in standard notation and tab, edited and performed on CD by virtuoso Paul Henry. Includes: Adelita • Capricho Árabe • Estudio Brillante • Grand Jota • Lágrima • Malagueña • María • Recuerdos de la Alhambra • Tango • and more, plus bios of Tárrega and Henry.

_______ 00698993 Book/CD Pack $19.99

Visit Hal Leonard Online at **www.halleonard.com**

Prices, contents and availability subject to change without notice.

0315